HEATHCLIFF DOES IT AGAIN!

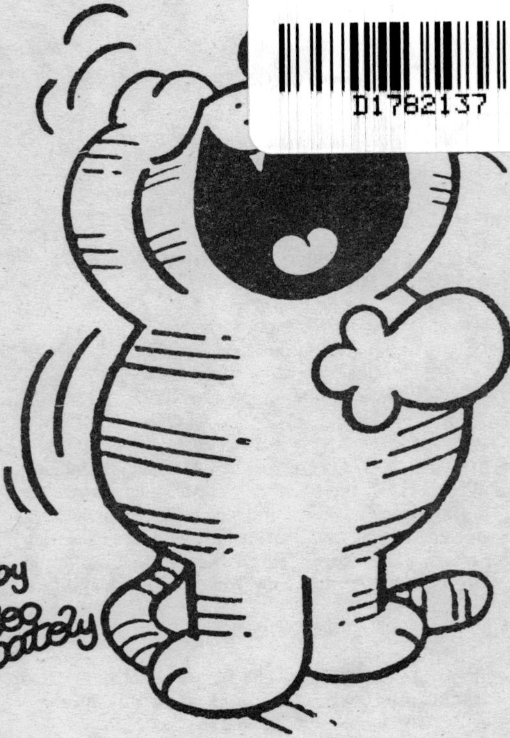

by

Geo Gately

J

JOVE BOOKS, NEW YORK

HEATHCLIFF DOES IT AGAIN!

A Jove Book / published by arrangement with
McNaught Syndicate, Inc.

PRINTING HISTORY
Tempo edition / January 1982
Charter edition / July 1984
Jove edition / September 1987

All rights reserved.
Copyright © 1974, 1975, 1976, 1982 by McNaught Syndicate, Inc.
Heathcliff® is a registered trademark of McNaught Syndicate, Inc.
This book may not be reproduced in whole or in part,
by mimeograph or any other means, without permission.
For information address: The Berkley Publishing Group,
200 Madison Avenue, New York, New York 10016.

ISBN: 0-515-09508-7

Jove Books are published by The Berkley Publishing Group,
200 Madison Avenue, New York, New York 10016.
The name "JOVE" and the "J" logo
are trademarks belonging to Jove Publications, Inc.

PRINTED IN THE UNITED STATES OF AMERICA

10 9 8 7 6 5 4 3 2

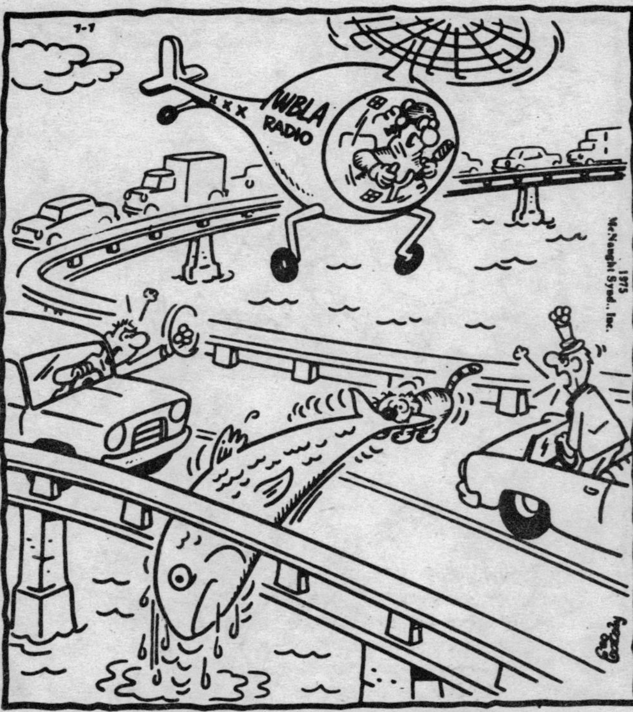
7-7
WBLA
RADIO
1975
McNaught Synd., Inc.

"TRAFFIC ON THE BAYVILLE BRIDGE IS ENCOUNTERING SOME DELAY..."

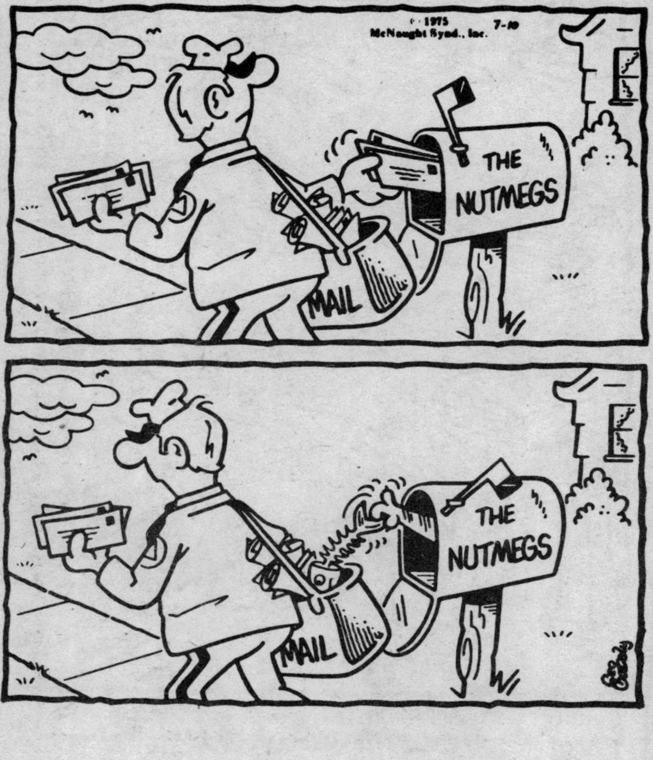
© 1975
McNaught Synd., Inc.
7-10
THE NUTMEGS
MAIL
THE NUTMEGS
MAIL

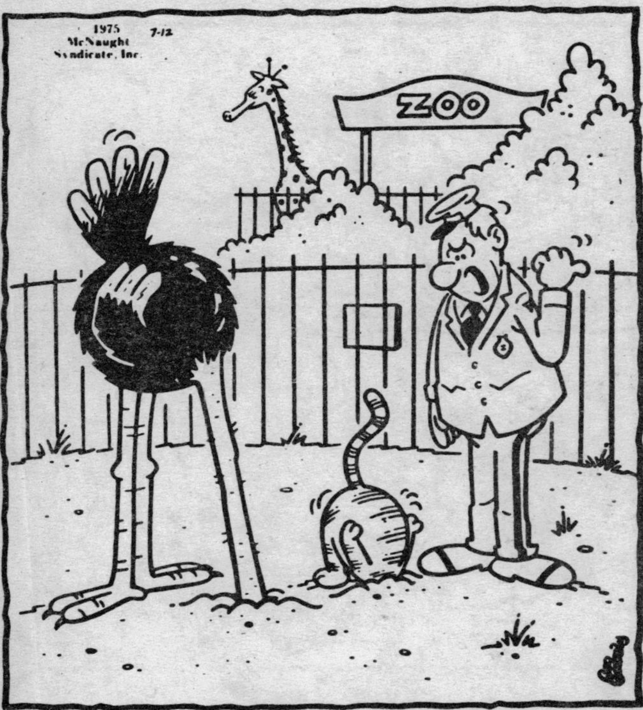
1975
McNaught
Syndicate, Inc.
7-12
ZOO

"NO VISITORS ALLOWED BEHIND THE FENCE!"

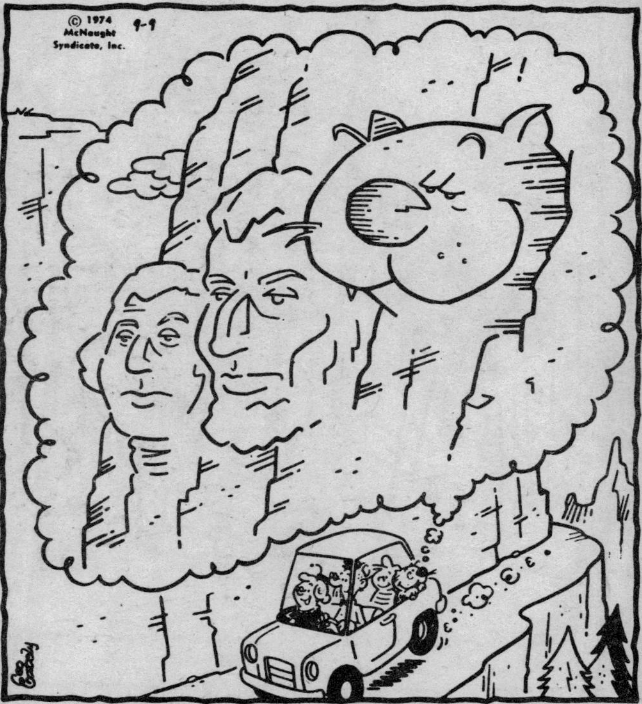

© 1974 McNaught Syndicate, Inc.
9-9

"HEATHCLIFF SEEMED TO ENJOY MOUNT RUSHMORE."

GRRRRRRR
© 1974 McNaught Synd., Inc.
9-10

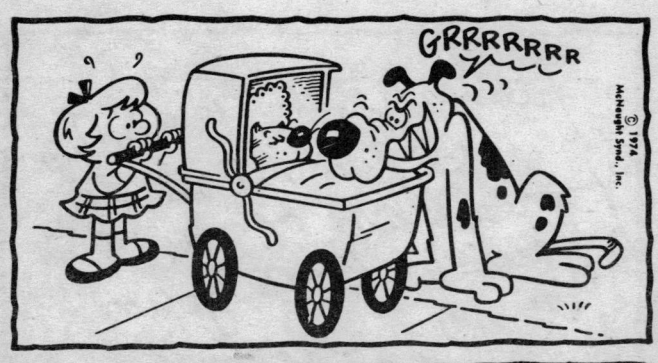

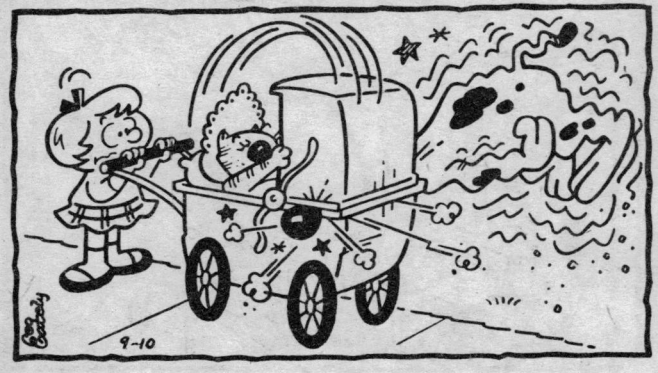

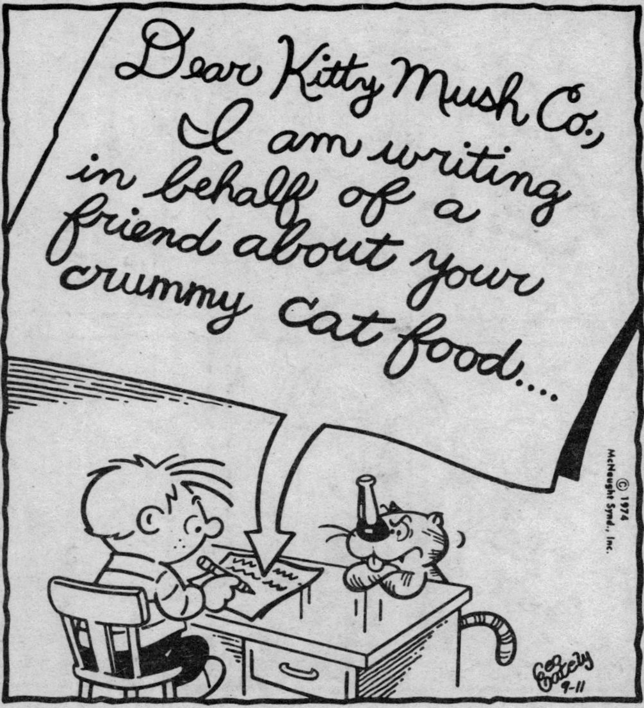
Dear Kitty Mush Co.,
I am writing in behalf of a friend about your crummy cat food....
© 1974 McNaught Synd., Inc.
Gately 9-11

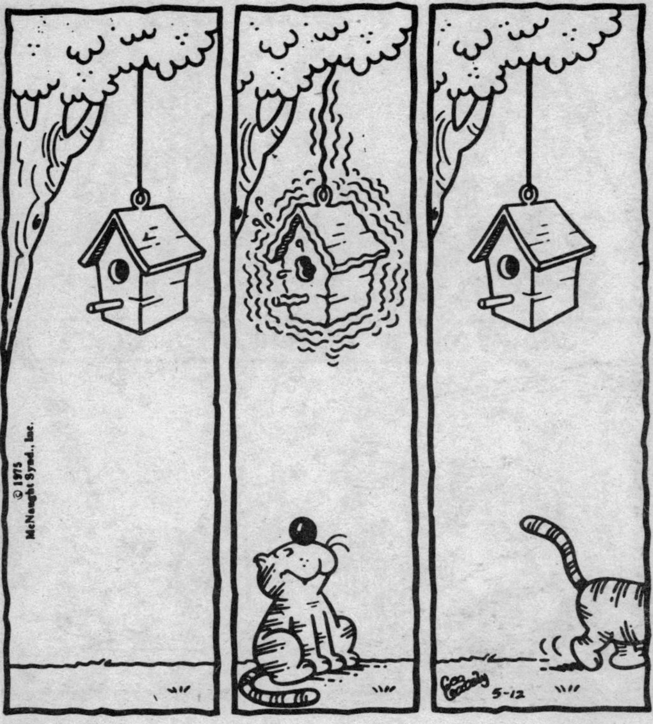

© 1975 McNaught Synd., Inc.
5-12

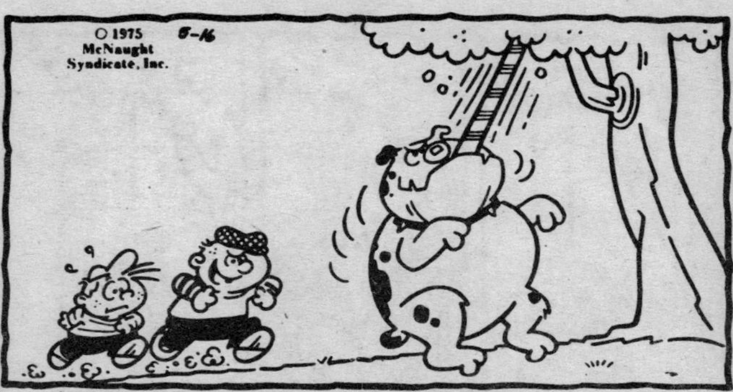
© 1975
McNaught
Syndicate, Inc.
5-16

"HAH!...MY DOG'S GOT OL' HEATHCLIFF THIS TIME!"

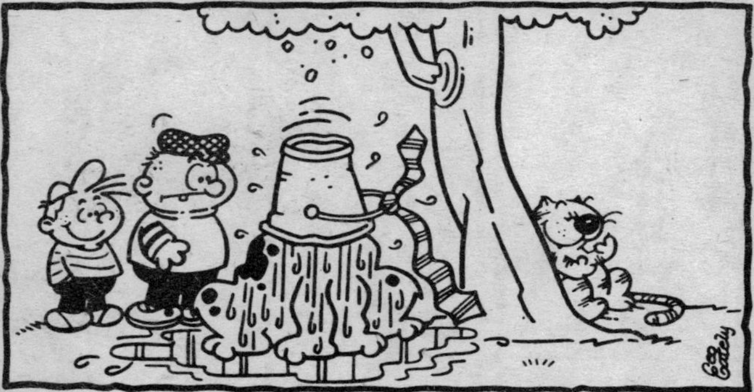
Geo Gately

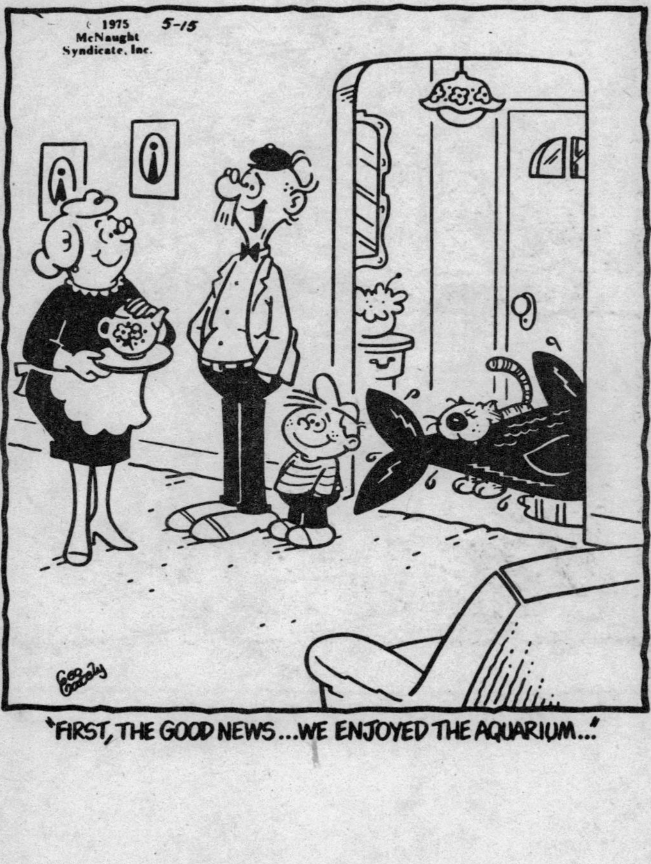

© 1975
McNaught
Syndicate, Inc.
5-15

"FIRST, THE GOOD NEWS...WE ENJOYED THE AQUARIUM..."

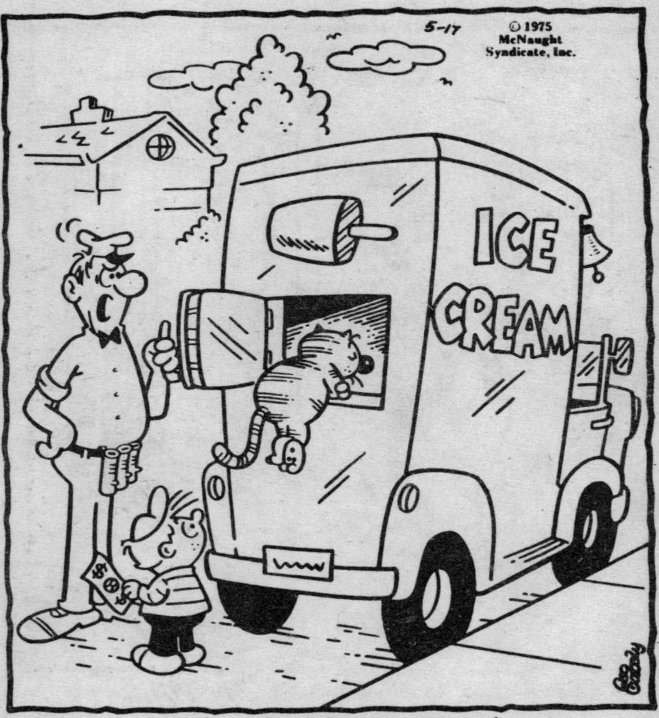

5-17
© 1975
McNaught
Syndicate, Inc.
ICE
CREAM

"SEE ANYTHING YOU LIKE?!!"

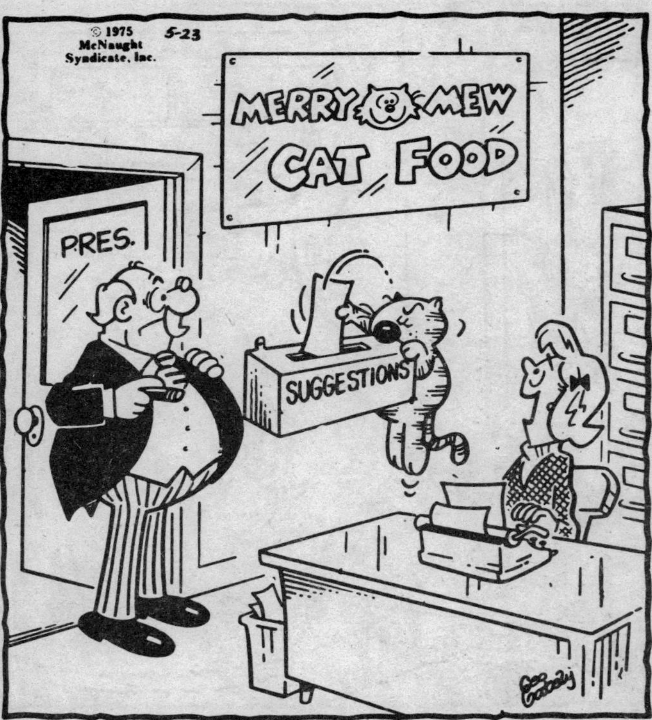
© 1975
McNaught
Syndicate, Inc.
5-23
MERRY MEW
CAT FOOD
PRES.
SUGGESTIONS

"EVERY NOW AND THEN HE STOPS BY."

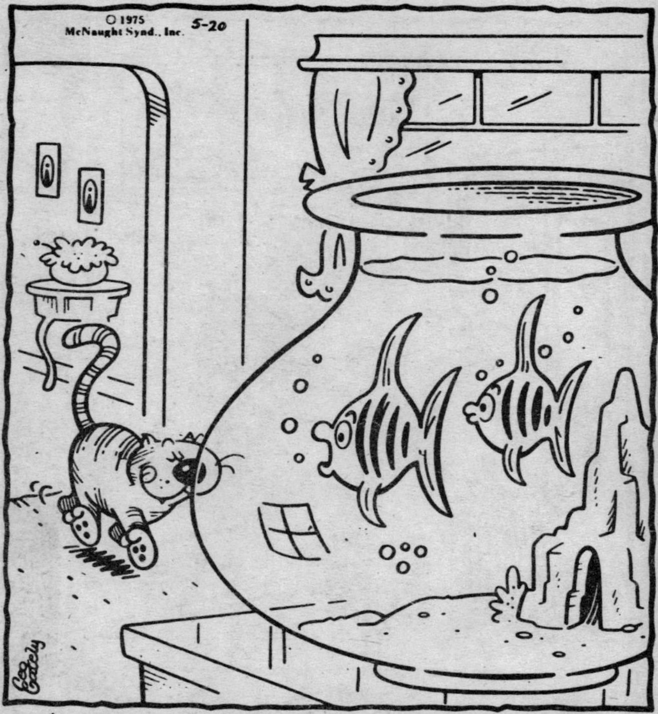
© 1975
McNaught Synd., Inc.
5-20
Geo Gately

"OH, OH!... HERE HE COMES... OL' STICKY FINGERS!"

TED
POST
OFFICE
WANTED
PO
OFF
1975
McNaught Synd., Inc. 5-22

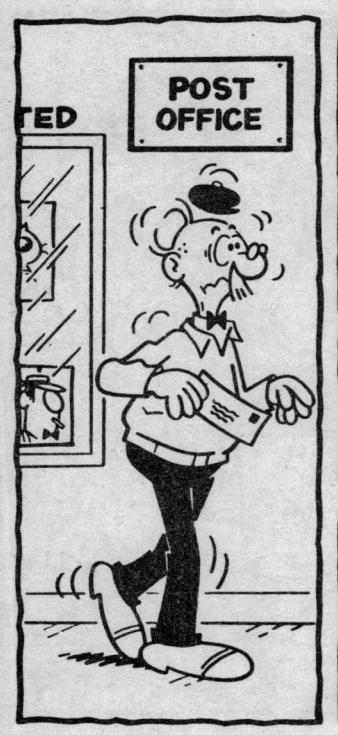

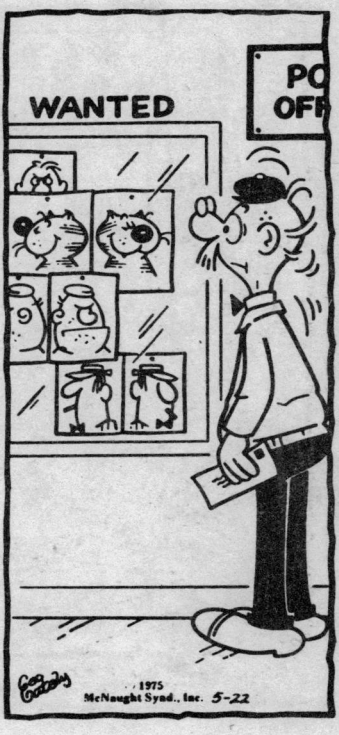

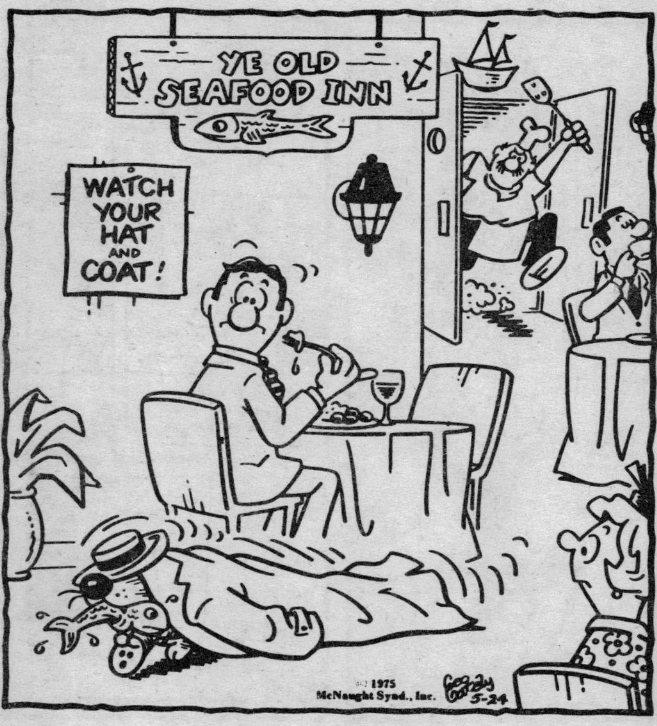
YE OLD SEAFOOD INN
WATCH YOUR HAT AND COAT!
© 1975 McNaught Synd., Inc.
5-24

1975 McNaught Synd., Inc.
7-25
HAIR RESTORER
"AH! JUST THE MAN I'M LOOKING FOR..."
HAIR RESTORER

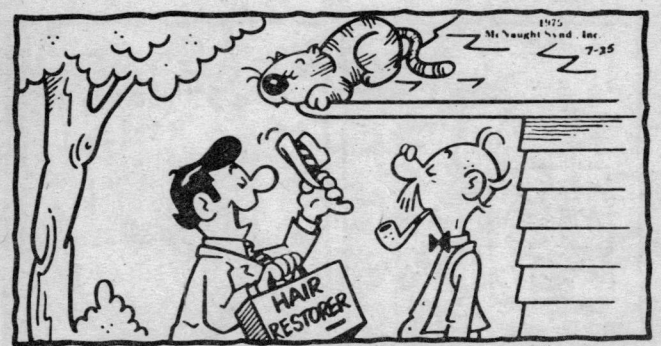

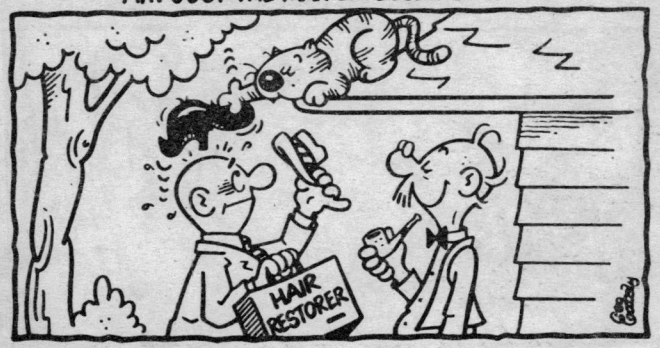

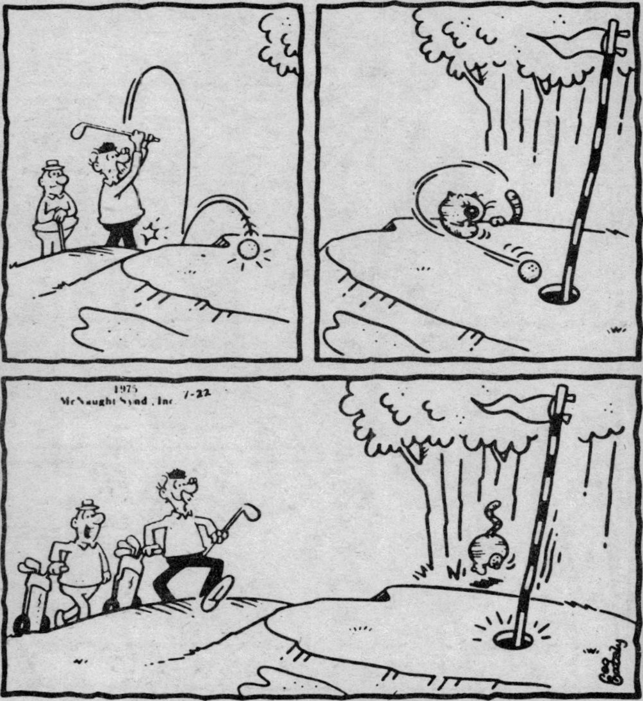
1975
McNaught Synd., Inc. 7-22

" YOUR GAME IS IMPROVING ! "

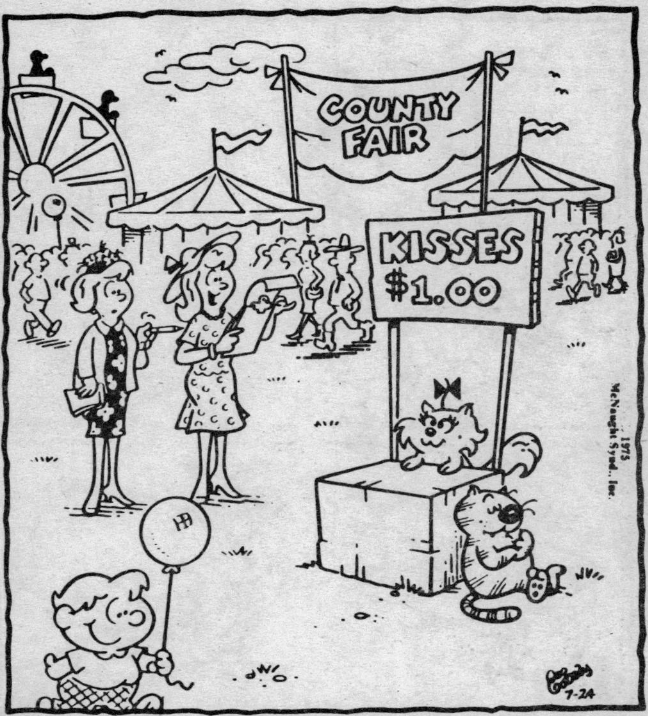
COUNTY FAIR
KISSES $1.00
1975 McNaught Synd., Inc.
7-24

"THAT LITTLE BOOTH WAS DONATED BY A MR. HEATHCLIFF NUTMEG."

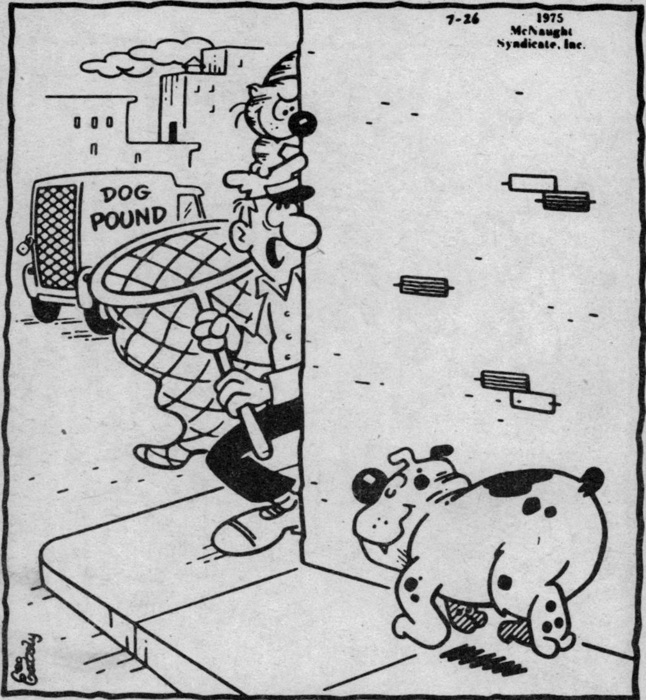
7-26
1975
McNaught
Syndicate, Inc.
DOG
POUND

"I'LL HANDLE THIS!"

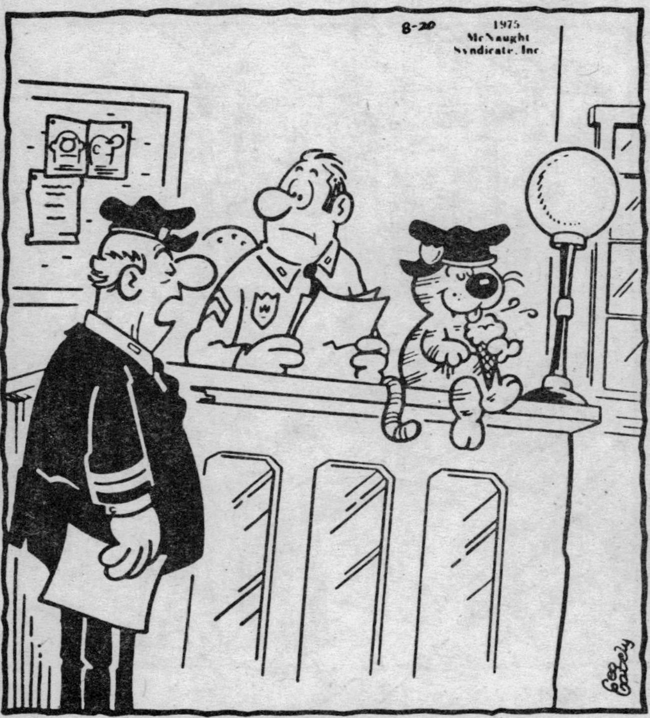
8-20
1975
McNaught
Syndicate, Inc.

"ARE YOU **SURE** HE'S LOST ?!"

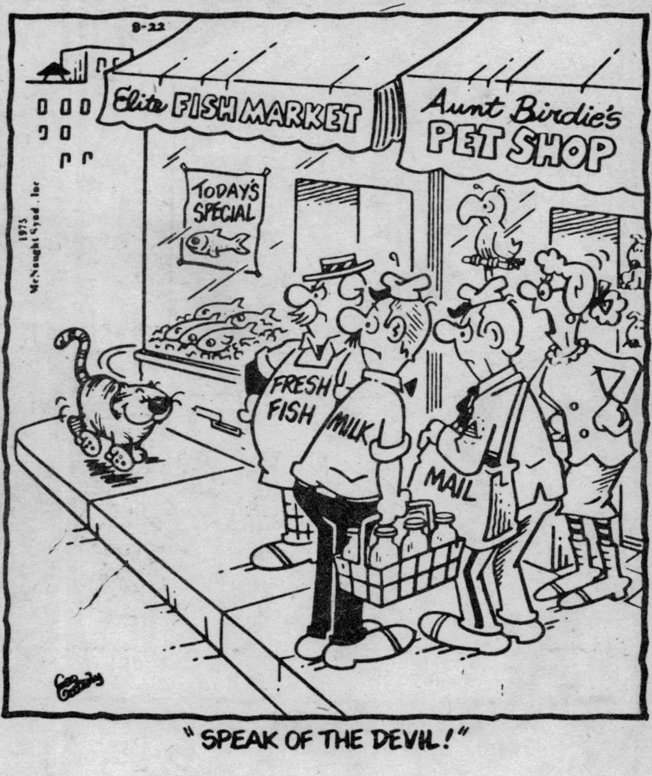
Elite FISH MARKET
Aunt Birdie's PET SHOP
TODAY'S SPECIAL
FRESH FISH
MILK
MAIL
8-22
1975 McNaught Synd., Inc

"SPEAK OF THE DEVIL!"

8-21
HEATHCLIFF
© 1975 McNaught Synd., Inc.

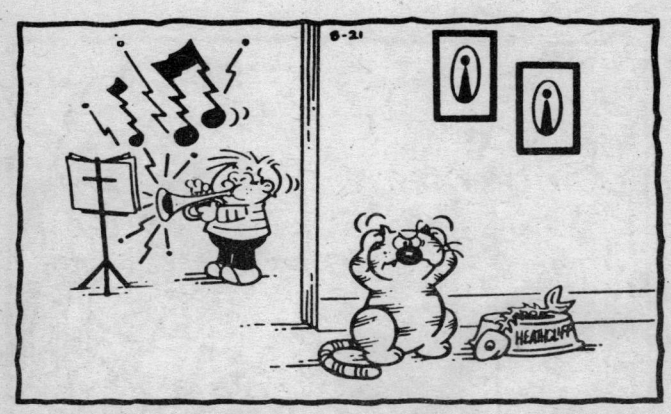

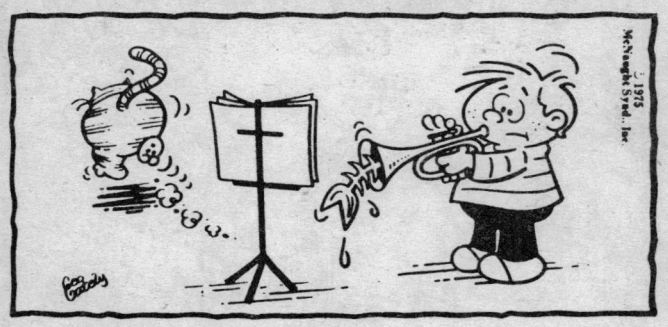

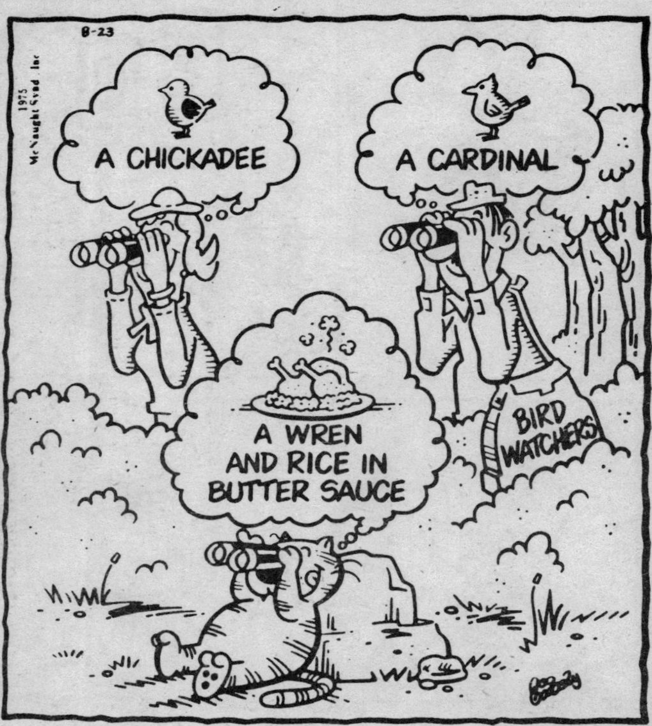
8-23
1975
McNaught Synd. Inc
A CHICKADEE
A CARDINAL
A WREN
AND RICE IN
BUTTER SAUCE
BIRD
WATCHERS

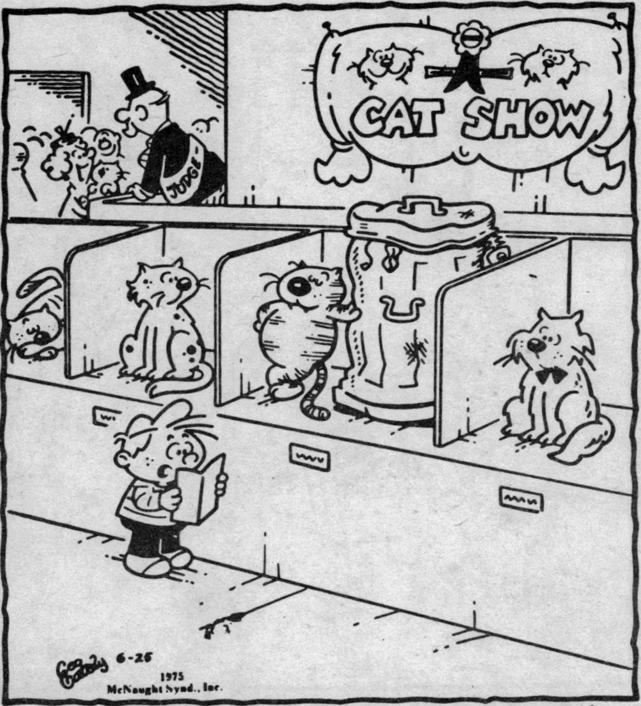
CAT SHOW
JUDGE
6-26
1975
McNaught Synd., Inc.
"THERE'S NO AWARD FOR 'BEST AT DUMPING GARBAGE CANS'."

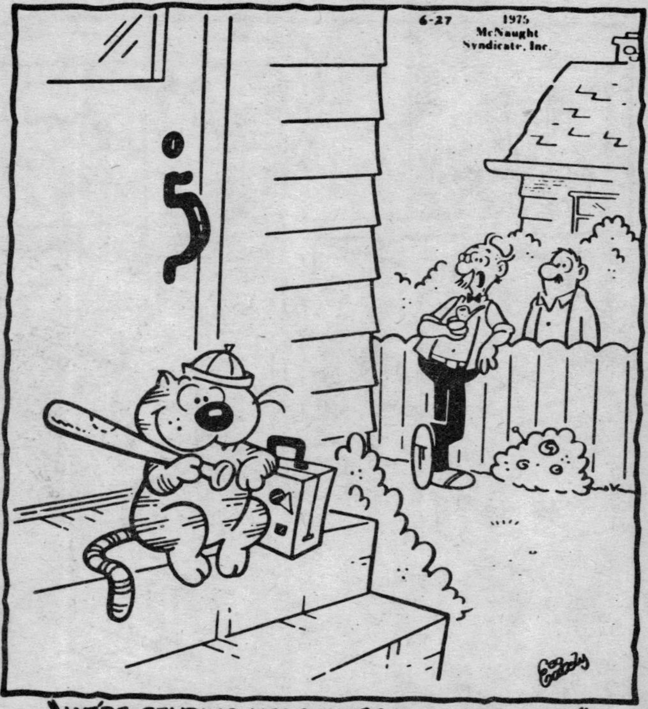
6-27
1975
McNaught
Syndicate, Inc.
"WE'RE SENDING HEATHCLIFF AWAY TO CAMP."

1975
McNaught
Syndicate, Inc.
6-24

"AND HOW ABOUT A NICE FLEA COLLAR FOR THE KITTY?" "THERE *ARE* NO FLEAS ON HEATHCLIFF!"

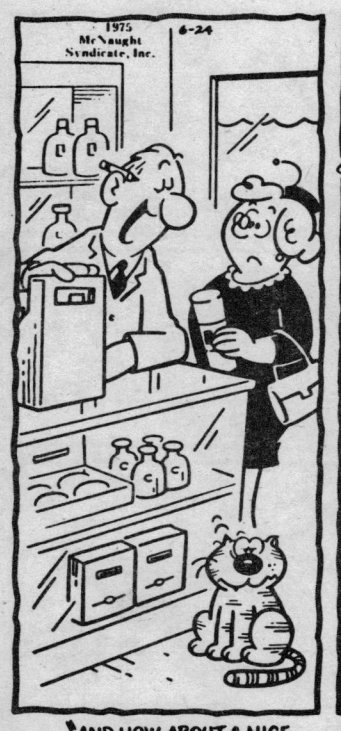

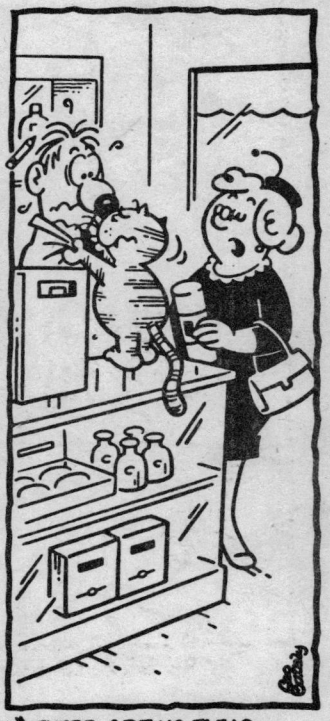

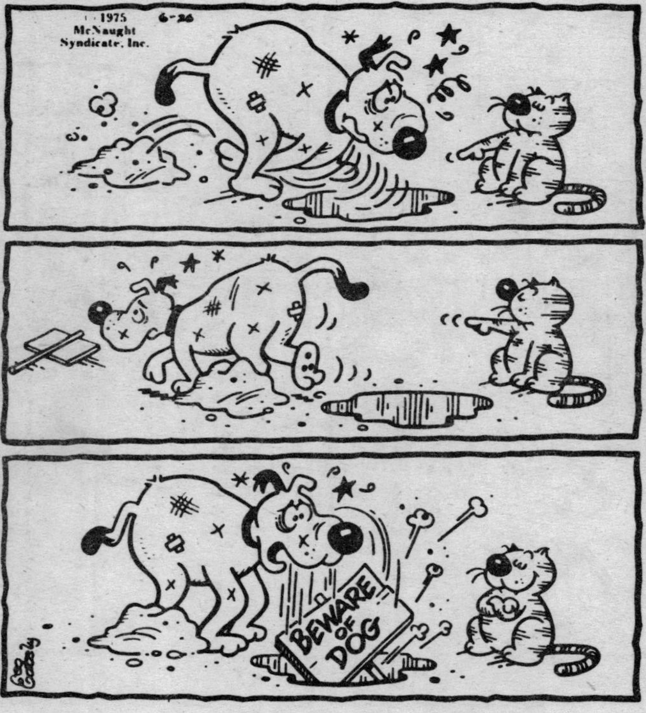
1975 6-26
McNaught
Syndicate, Inc.
BEWARE OF DOG

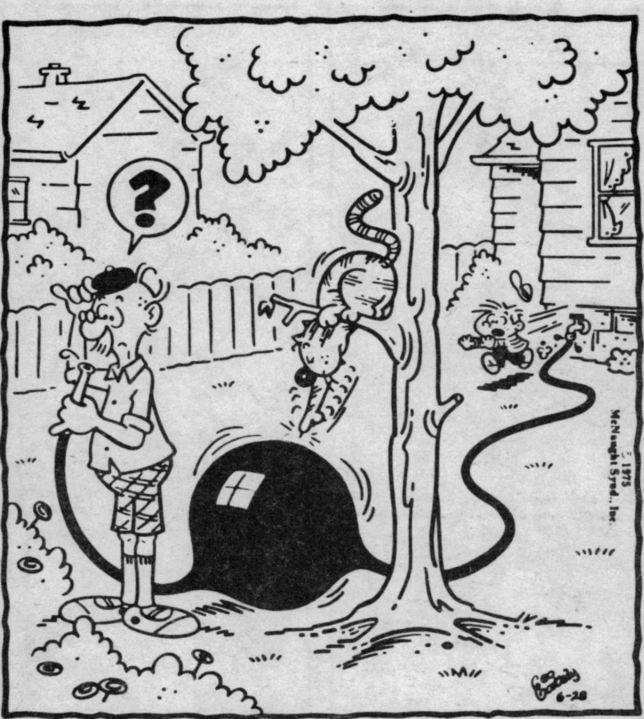
?
© 1975 McNaught Synd., Inc.

"HEATHCLIFF!...DON'T!"

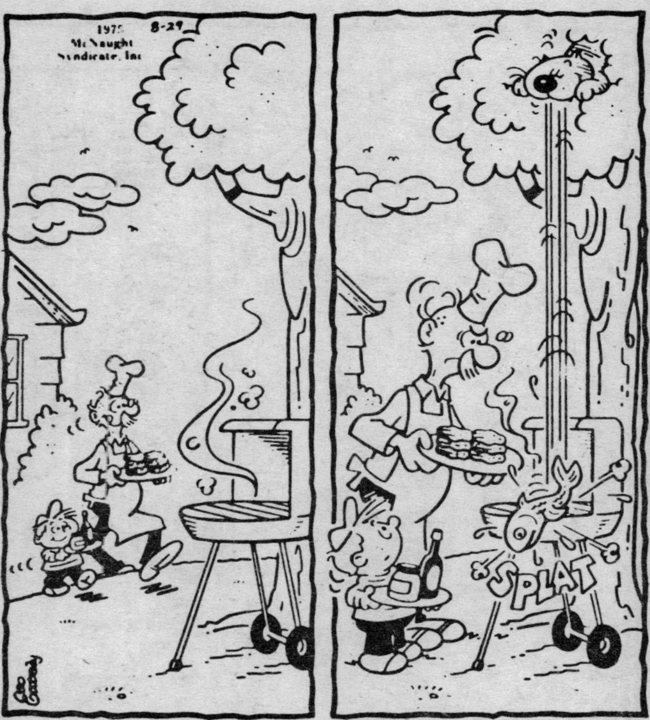
1975 McNaught Syndicate, Inc
8-29
SPLAT

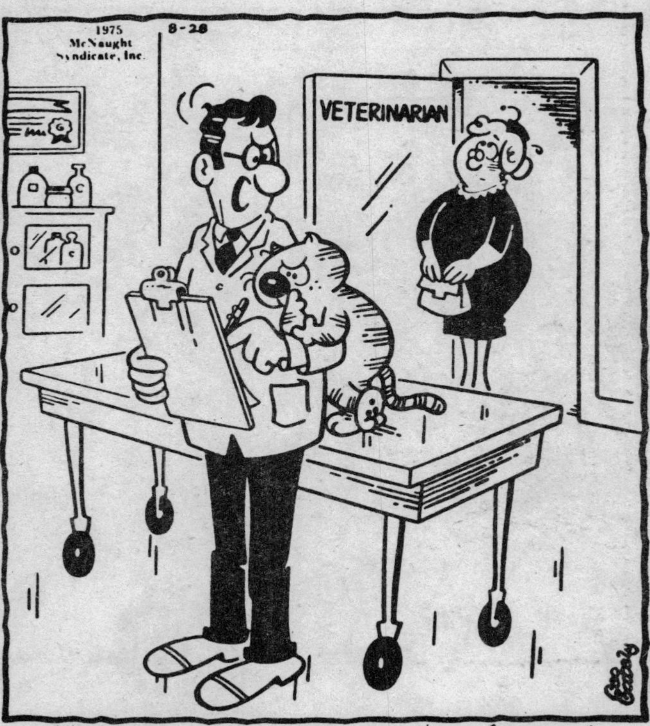
1975
McNaught
Syndicate, Inc.
8-28
VETERINARIAN

"I'LL MAKE THE DIAGNOSIS, IF YOU DON'T MIND!"

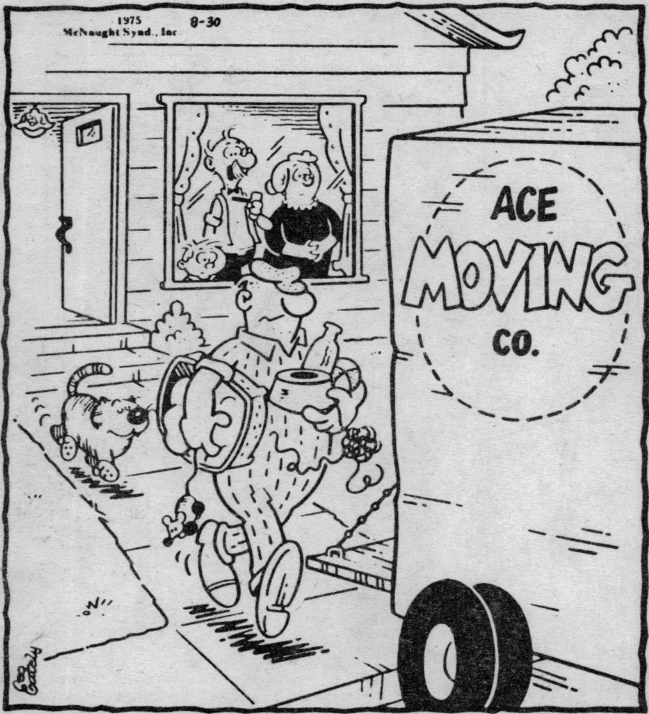
1975
McNaught Synd., Inc
8-30
ACE
MOVING
CO.

"HEATHCLIFF'S ***REALLY*** LEAVING HOME THIS TIME!"

9-26
1975
McNaught
Syndicate, Inc.
VETERINARIAN

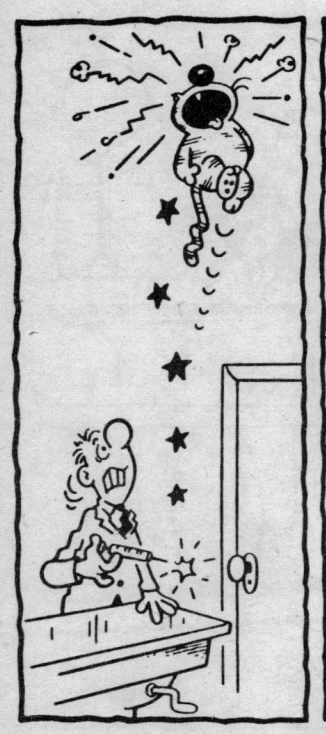

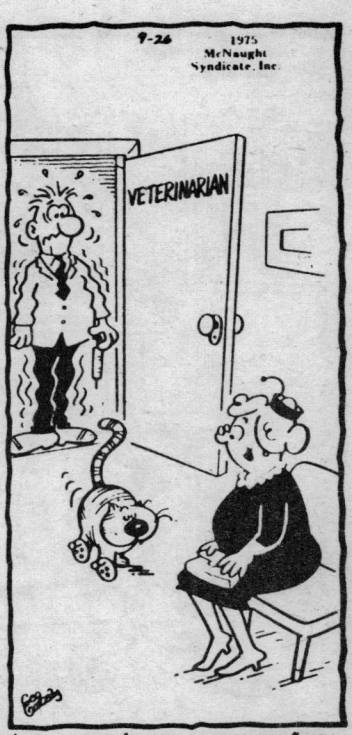

"AH!...THERE'S MY BRAVE BOY!!"

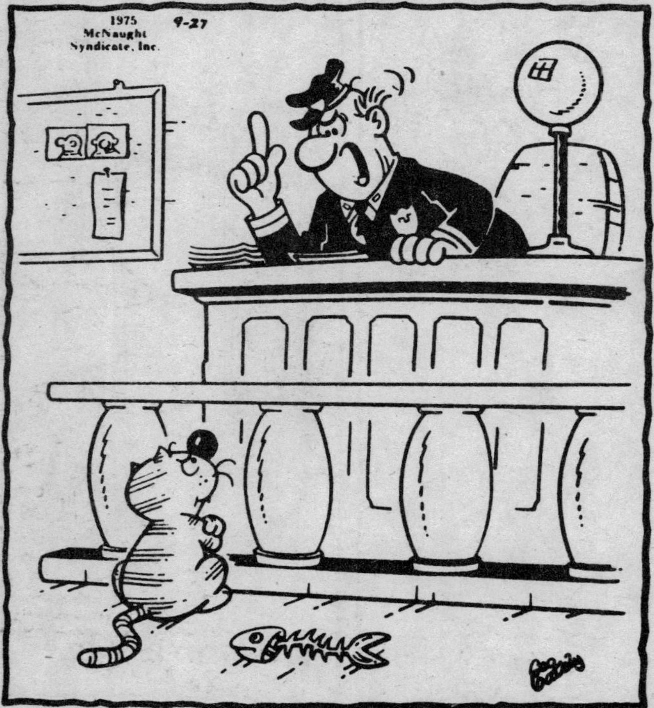
1975
McNaught
Syndicate, Inc.
9-27

"YOU'RE ALLOWED ONE PHONE CALL AND QUIT HISSING!"

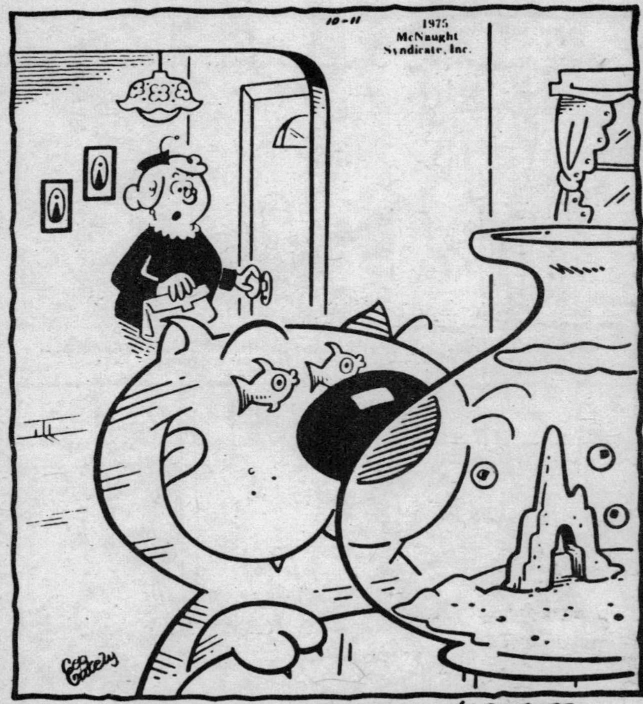
10-11
1975
McNaught
Syndicate, Inc.

"NOW, BE A GOOD KITTY AND DON'T BOTHER THOSE FISH WHILE I'M GONE!"

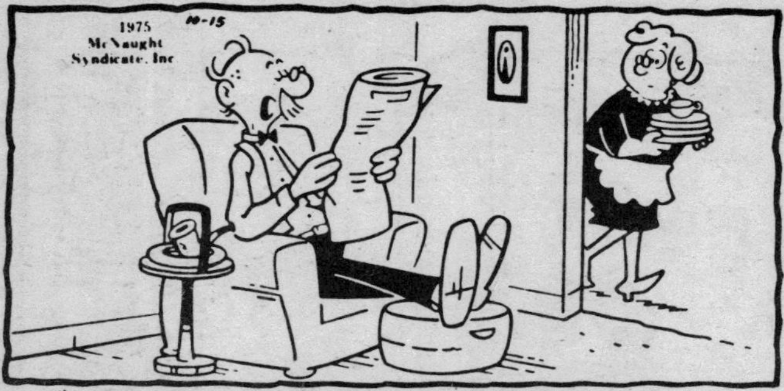
1975
McNaught
Syndicate, Inc
10-15

"LISTEN TO THIS...'WIDOW LEAVES ONE MILLION DOLLARS TO HER CAT'... NOW, ISN'T THAT RIDICULOUS ?!"

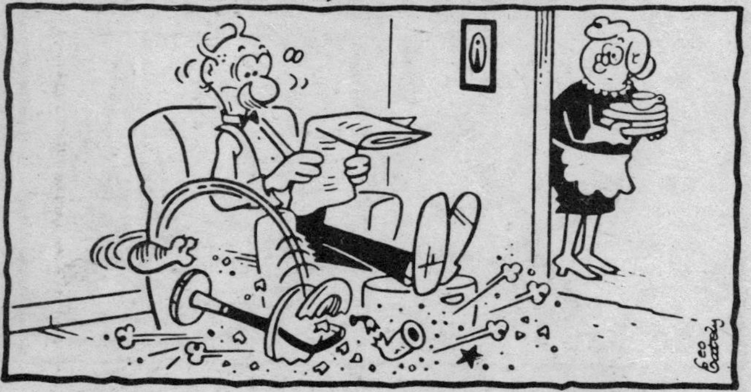

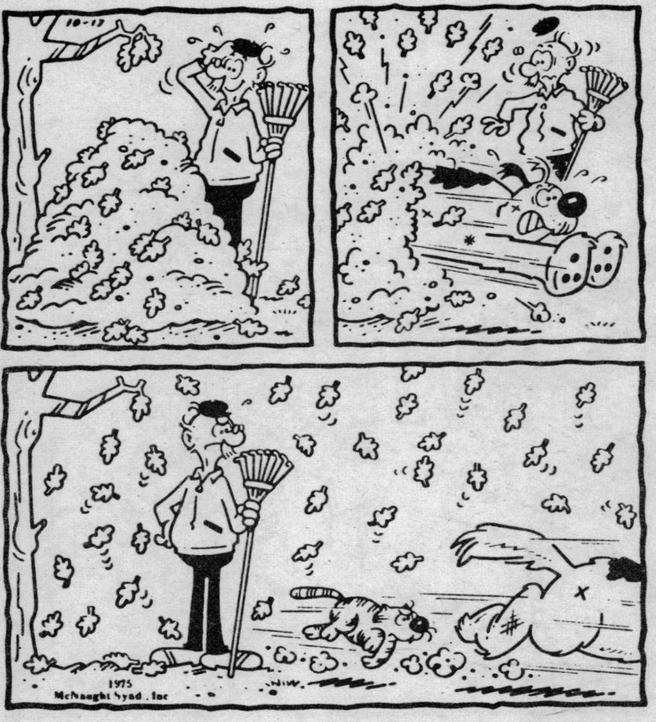
10-17
1975
McNaught Synd., Inc
NIW

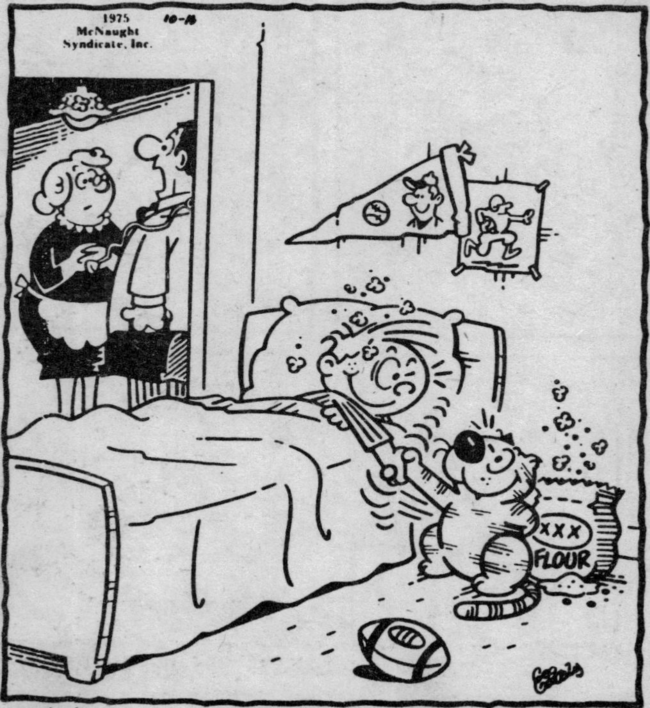
1975
McNaught
Syndicate, Inc.
XXX
FLOUR

"I'D KEEP HIM OUT OF SCHOOL FOR A FEW DAYS...
HE LOOKS A LITTLE PALE."

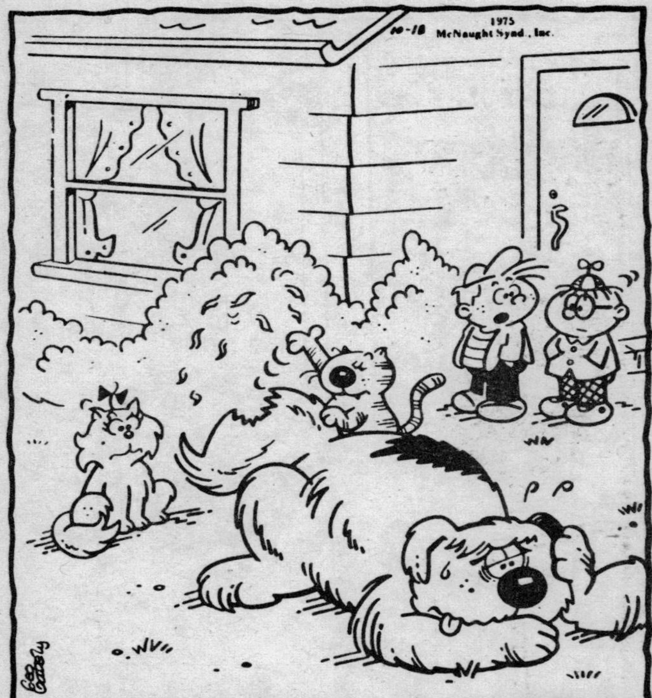
10-18
1975
McNaught Synd., Inc.

"I THINK HE'S DOING 'SHE LOVES ME, SHE LOVES ME NOT'!"

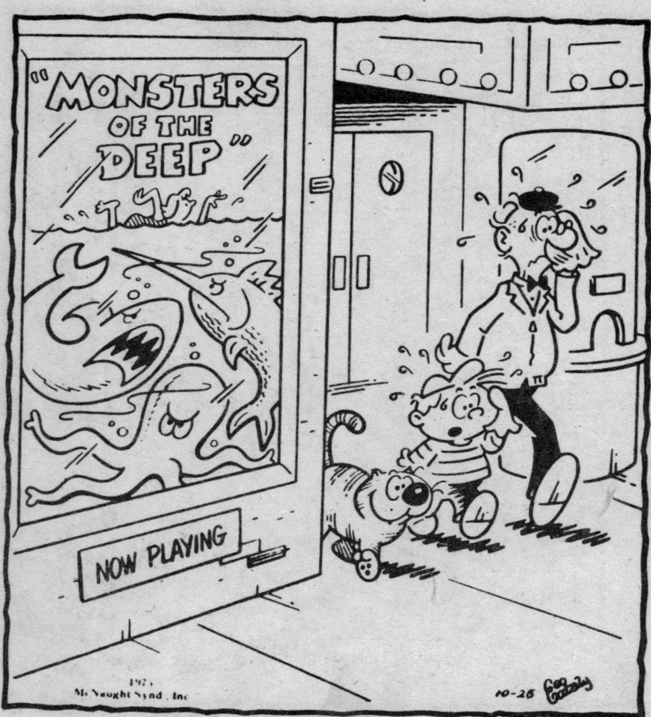
"MONSTERS OF THE DEEP"
NOW PLAYING
McNaught Synd., Inc.
10-25

"HEATHCLIFF LOVED IT!"

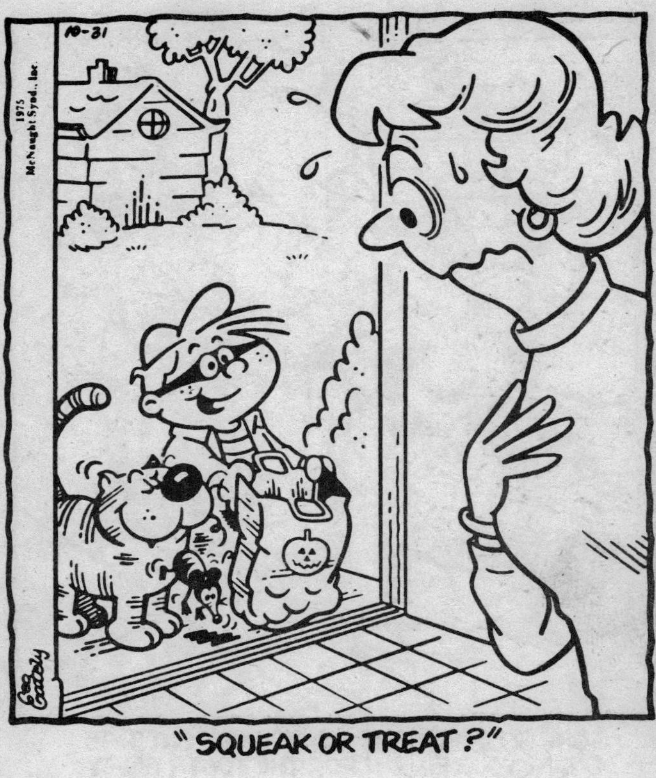
10-31
1975
McNaught Synd., Inc.

"SQUEAK OR TREAT?"

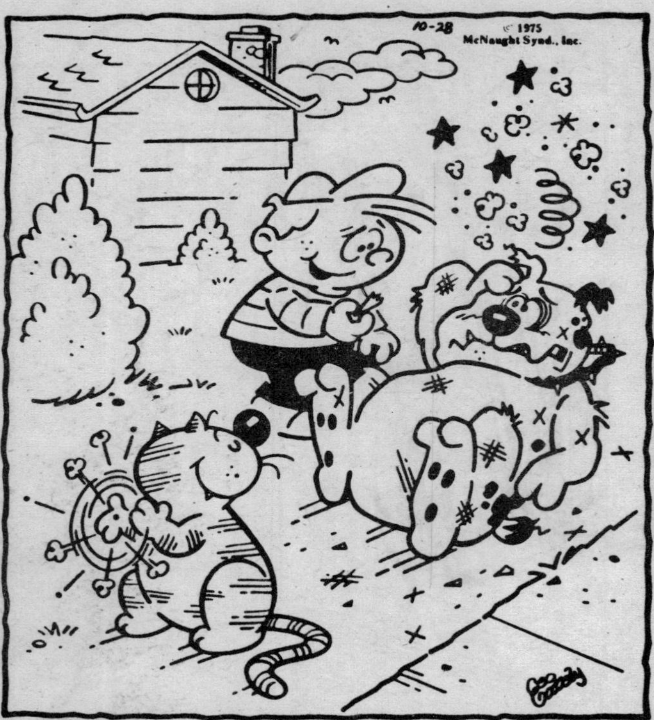
10-28
© 1975
McNaught Synd., Inc.

"ONE GOOD THING, SPIKE...YOU CAN PUT THIS UNDER YOUR PILLOW FOR THE TOOTH FAIRY!"

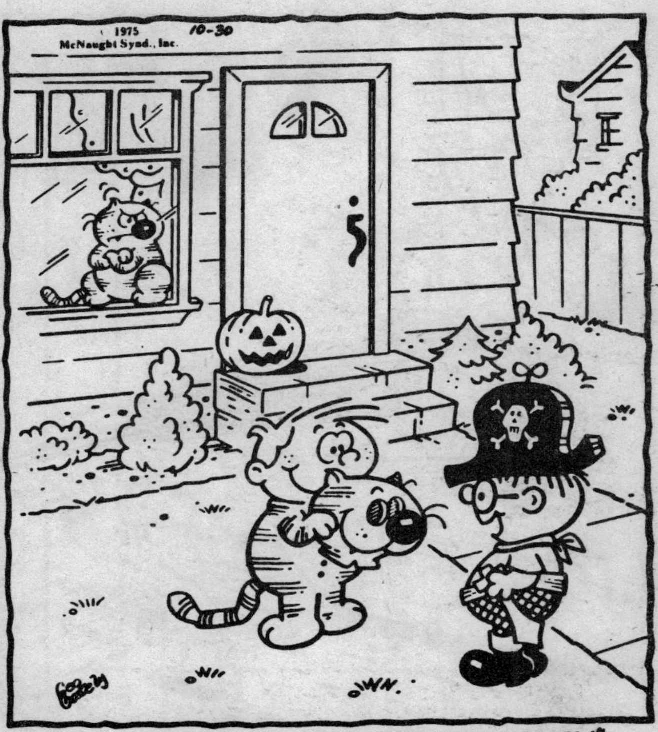

© 1975
McNaught Synd., Inc.
10-30

"WOW!...YOUR GRANDMA MAKES GREAT COSTUMES!"

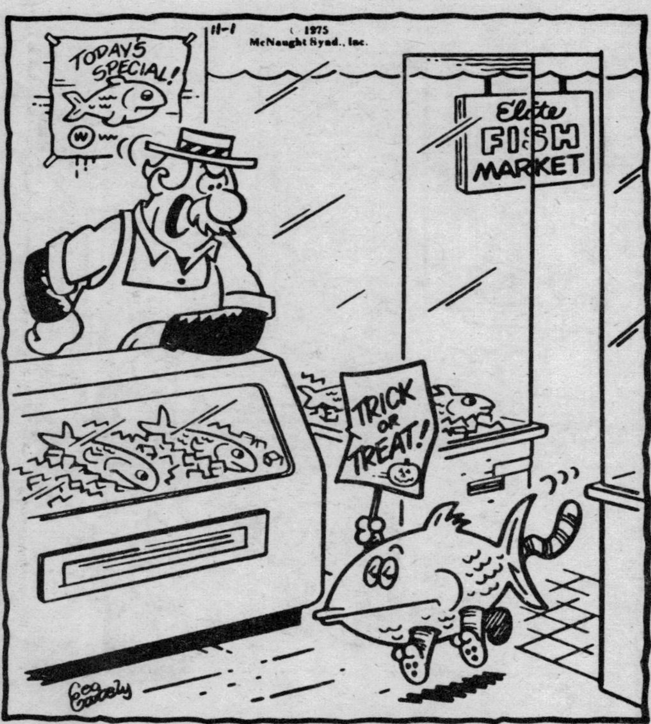
11-1
© 1975
McNaught Synd., Inc.
TODAY'S SPECIAL!
Elite
FISH
MARKET
TRICK OR TREAT!
Geo Gately

"HALLOWEEN WAS YESTERDAY, HEATHCLIFF!"

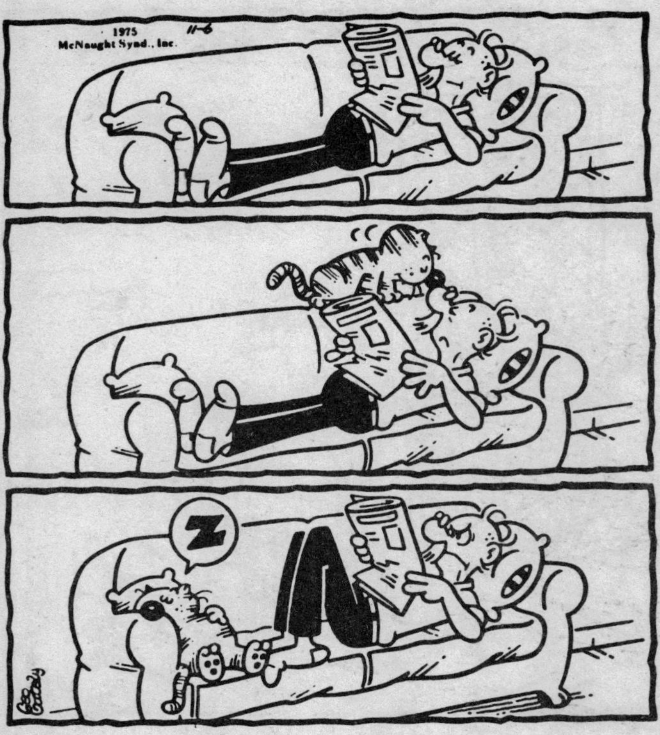
1975
McNaught Synd., Inc.
11-6
Z

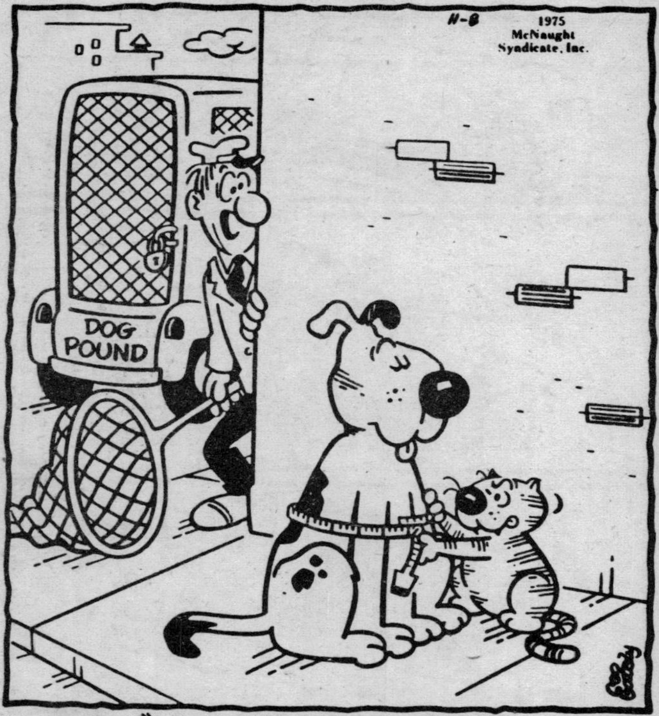

H-8
1975
McNaught
Syndicate, Inc.
DOG
POUND

"WILL HE FIT IN THE NET?"

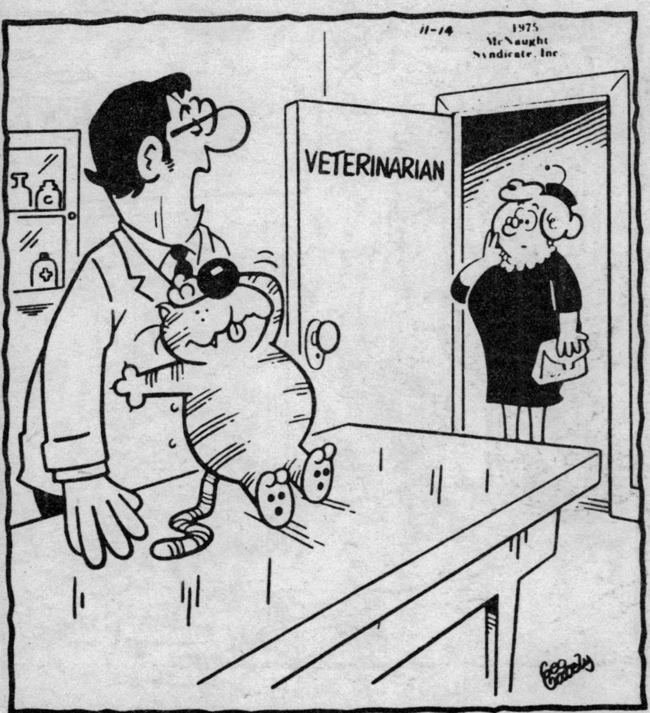

11-14
1975
McNaught
Syndicate, Inc.
VETERINARIAN

"HE'S A BIT OF A HYPOCHONDRIAC, ISN'T HE?"

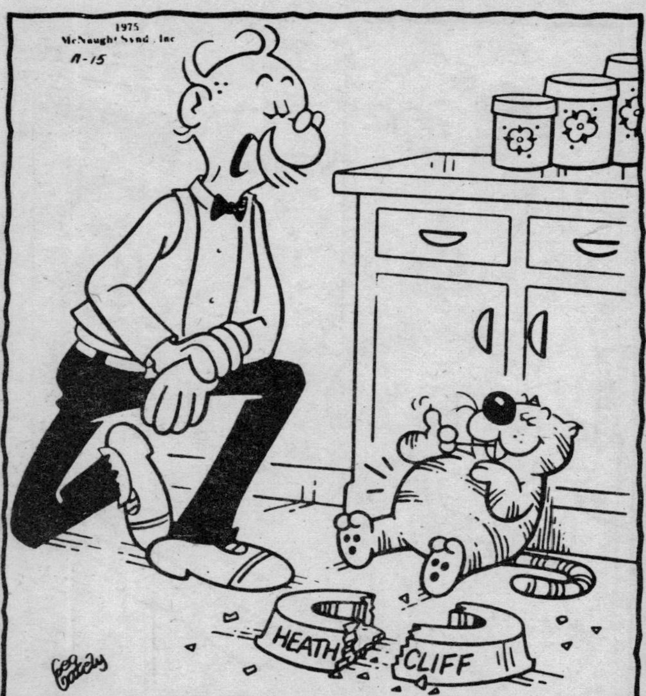
1975
McNaught Synd., Inc
HEATH
CLIFF

"ARE YOU AWARE THAT MANY CATS ARE FINICKY EATERS?"

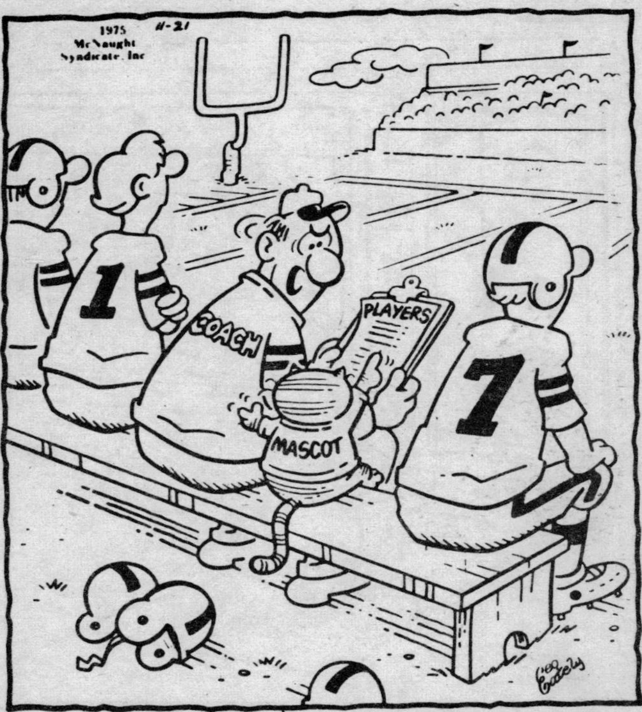
1975
McNaught
Syndicate, Inc
11-21
COACH
PLAYERS
MASCOT
1
7

"IF YOU DON'T MIND, I'LL DECIDE WHO TO SEND IN!!"

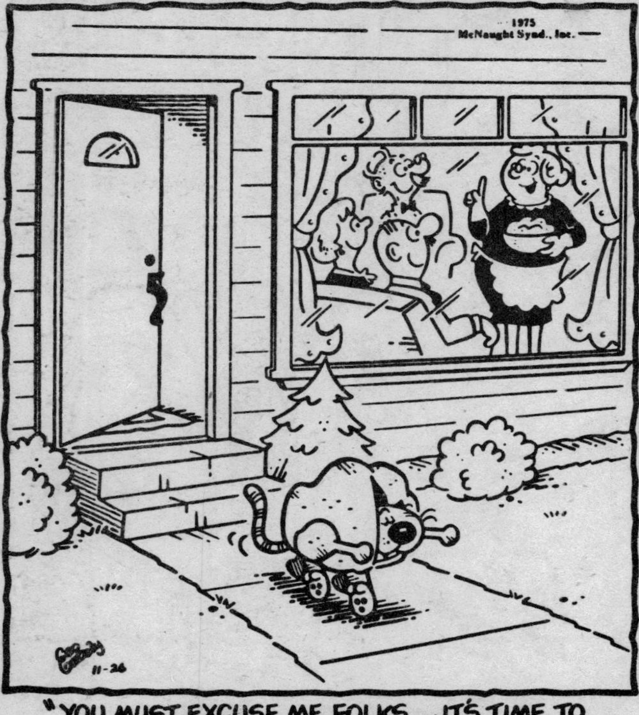
1975
McNaught Synd., Inc.
11-26

"YOU MUST EXCUSE ME, FOLKS... IT'S TIME TO STUFF THE TURKEY."

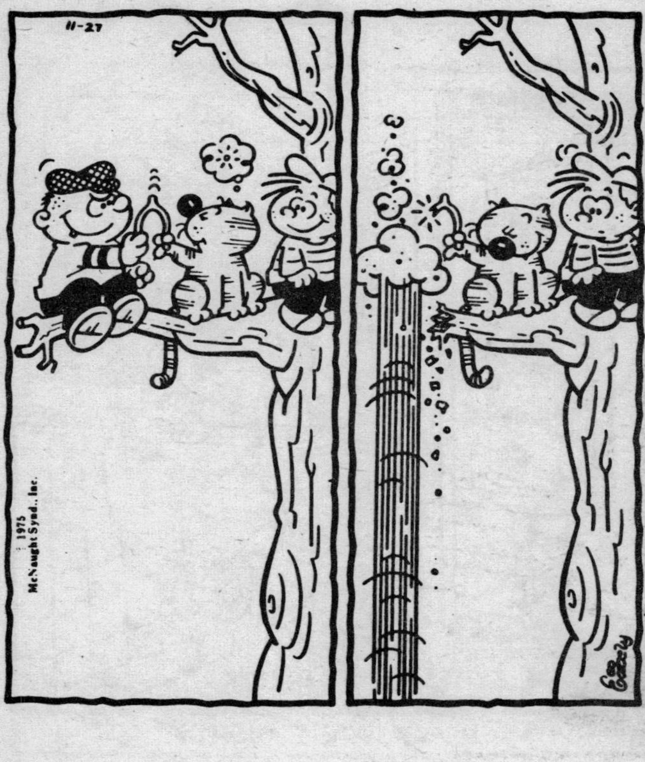
11-27
© 1975
McNaught Synd., Inc.

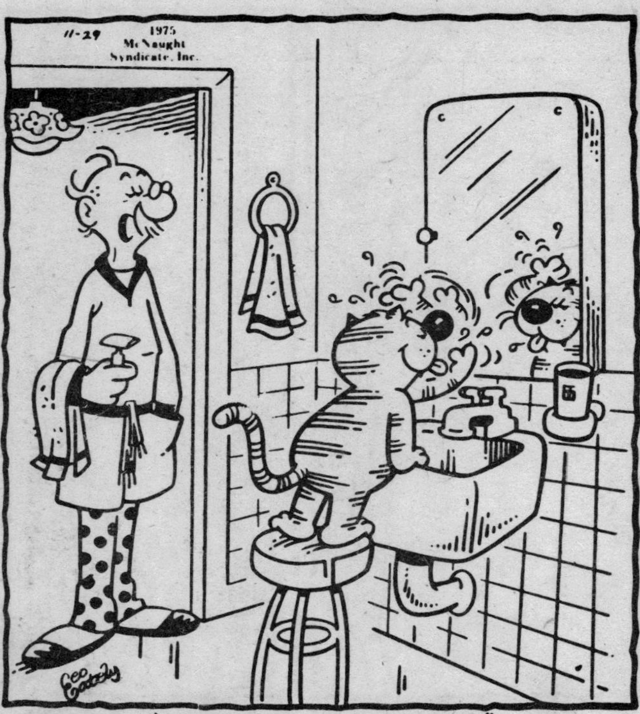
11-29
1975
McNaught
Syndicate, Inc.

"HEAVY DATE TONIGHT?"

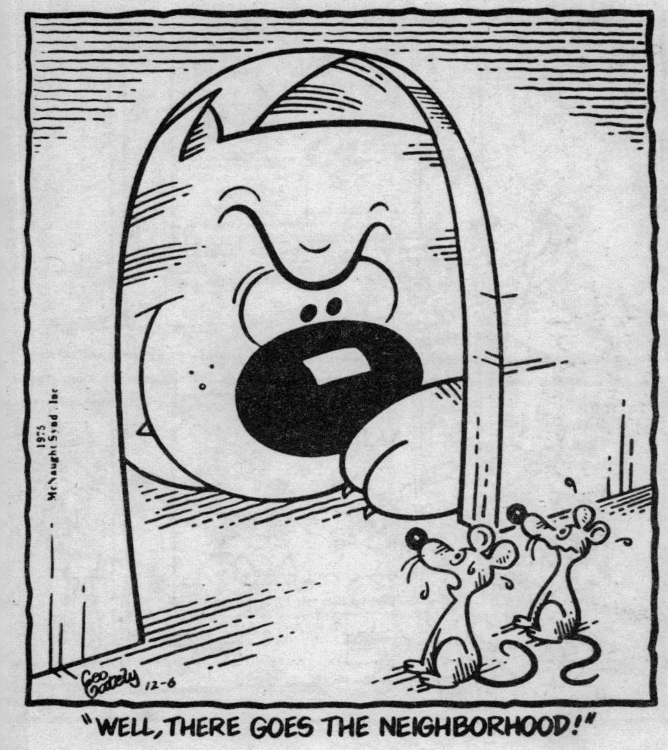

"WELL, THERE GOES THE NEIGHBORHOOD!"

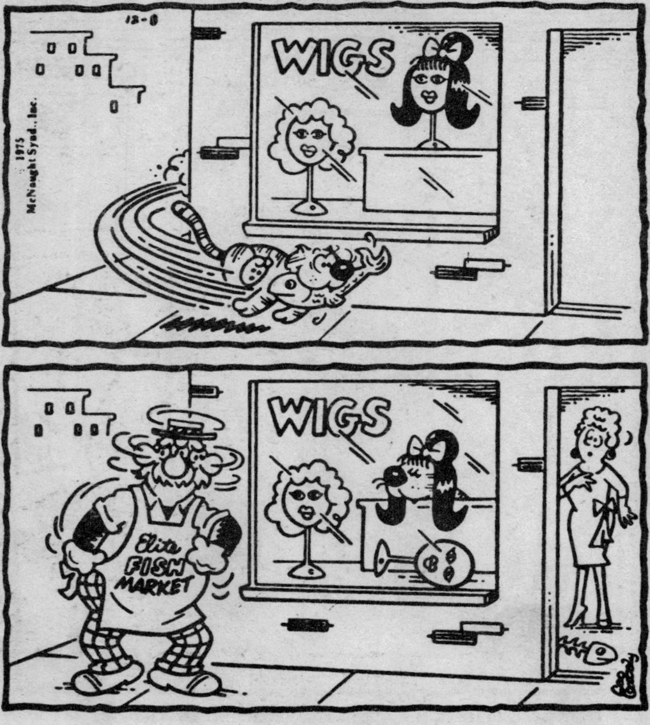
12-8
1975
McNaught Synd., Inc.
WIGS
WIGS
Elite
FISH
MARKET

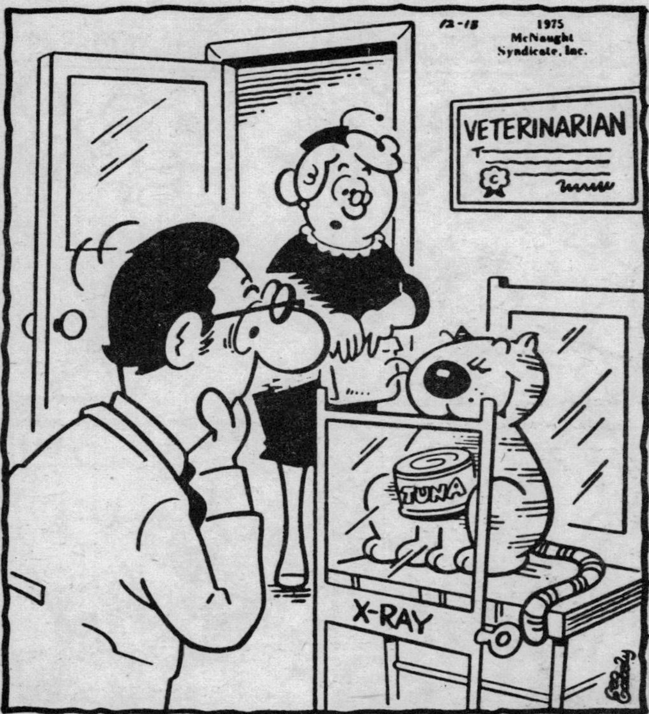
12-15
1975
McNaught
Syndicate, Inc.
VETERINARIAN
TUNA
X-RAY

"WELL, YES...HE DOES HAVE A TENDENCY TO BOLT HIS FOOD."

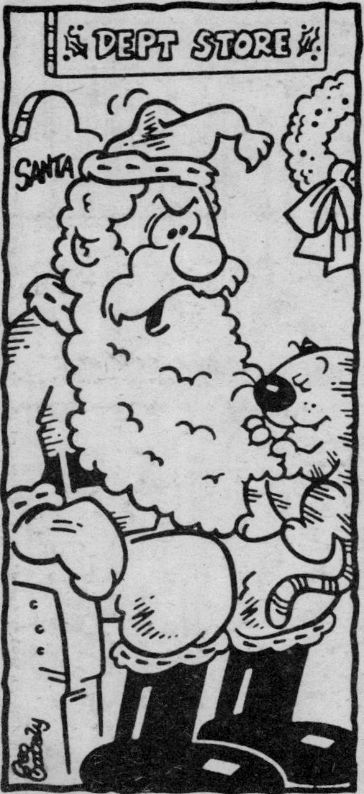
DEPT STORE
SANTA

"NO CATS ALLOWED!"

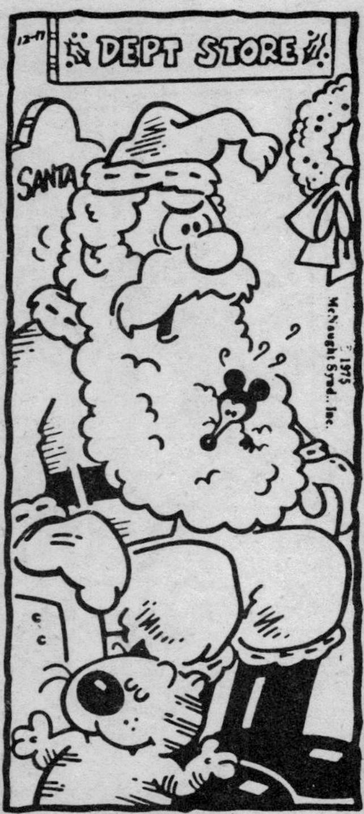
12-17
DEPT STORE
SANTA
© 1975 McNaught Synd., Inc.

"NEXT!"

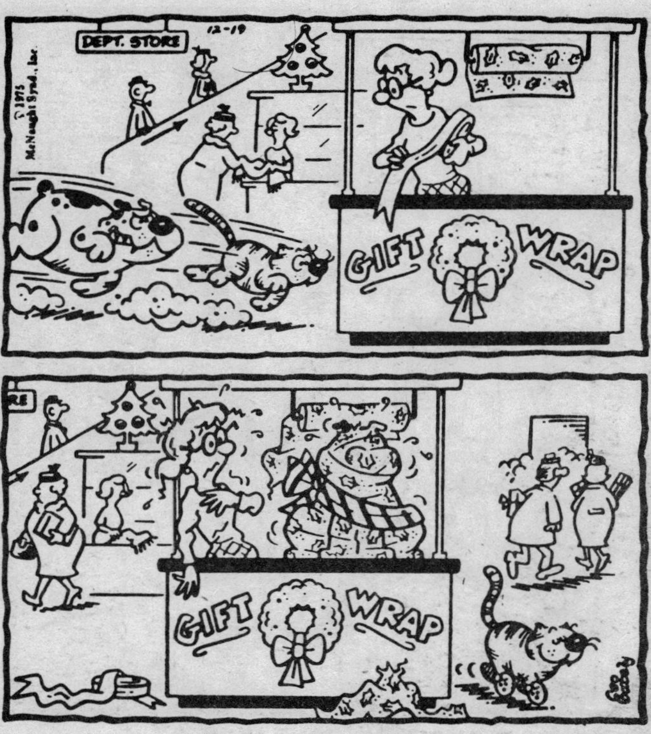
DEPT. STORE
12-19
©1975 McNaught Synd., Inc.
GIFT
WRAP
GIFT
WRAP

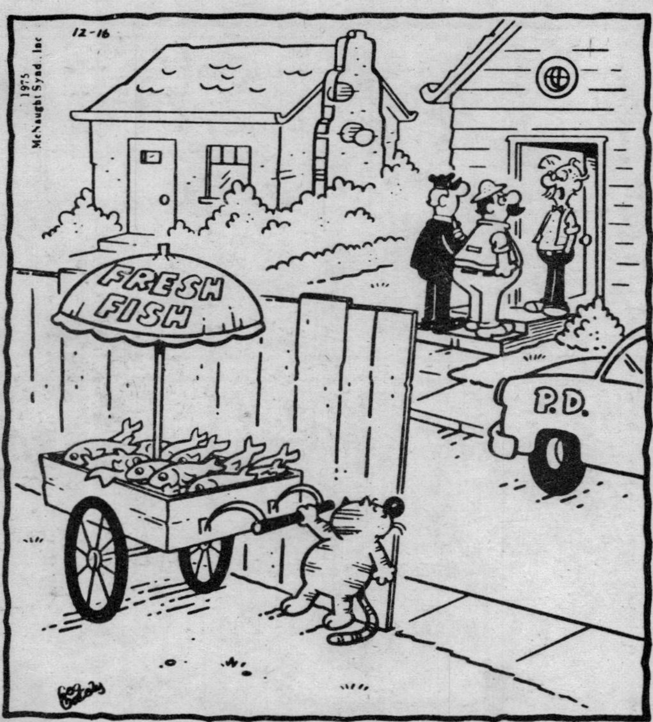
12-16
1975 McNaught Synd., Inc
FRESH FISH
P.D.

"WHAT'S HE DONE NOW ?!"

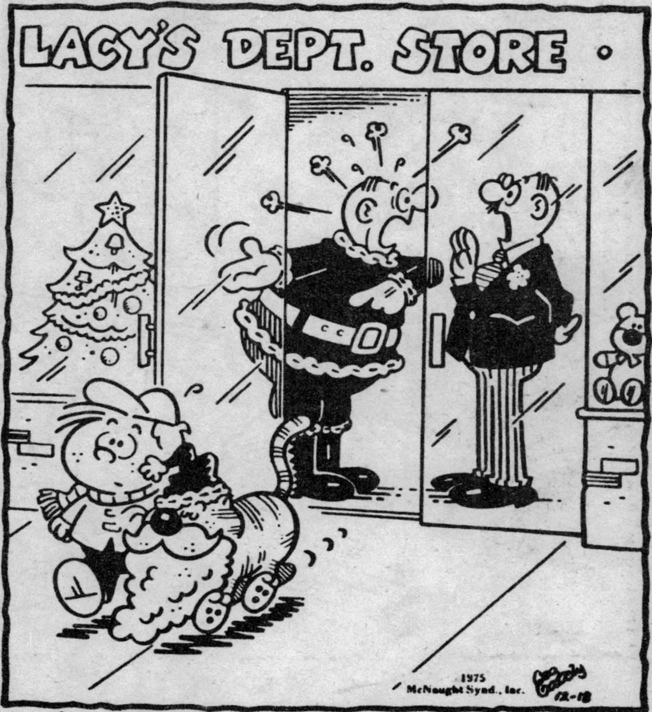
LACY'S DEPT. STORE
1975
McNaught Synd., Inc.
12-18

"CALM DOWN AND TELL ME WHAT HAPPENED!"

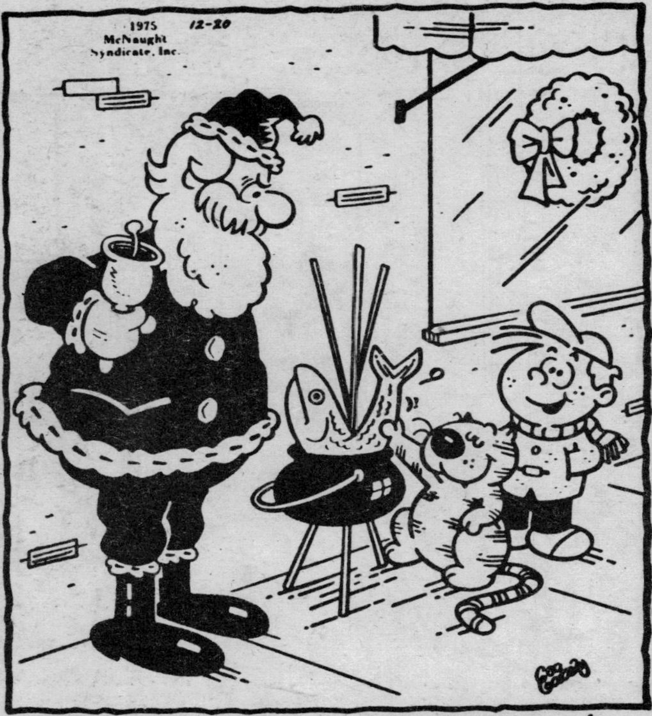
1975 McNaught Syndicate, Inc.
12-20

"HE WANTS YOU TO GIVE IT TO A NEEDY CAT."

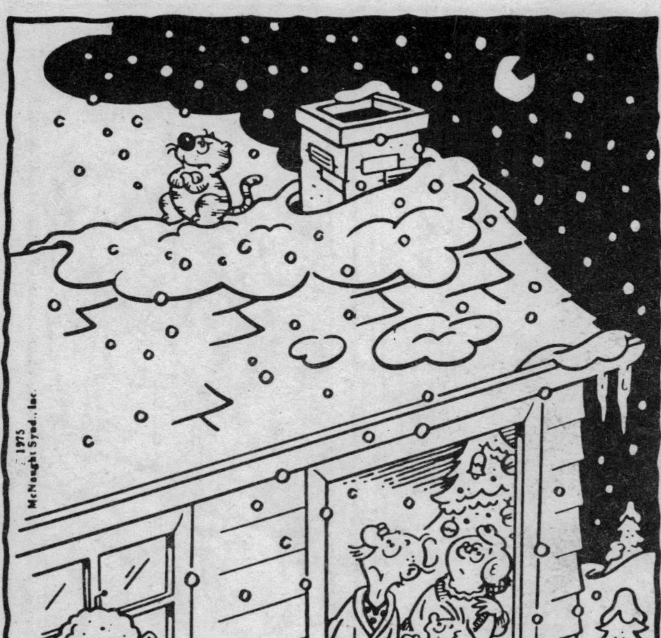
© 1975 McNaught Synd., Inc.
12-24

"HEATHCLIFF DOESN'T LIKE THE IDEA OF REINDEER LANDING ON OUR ROOF!"

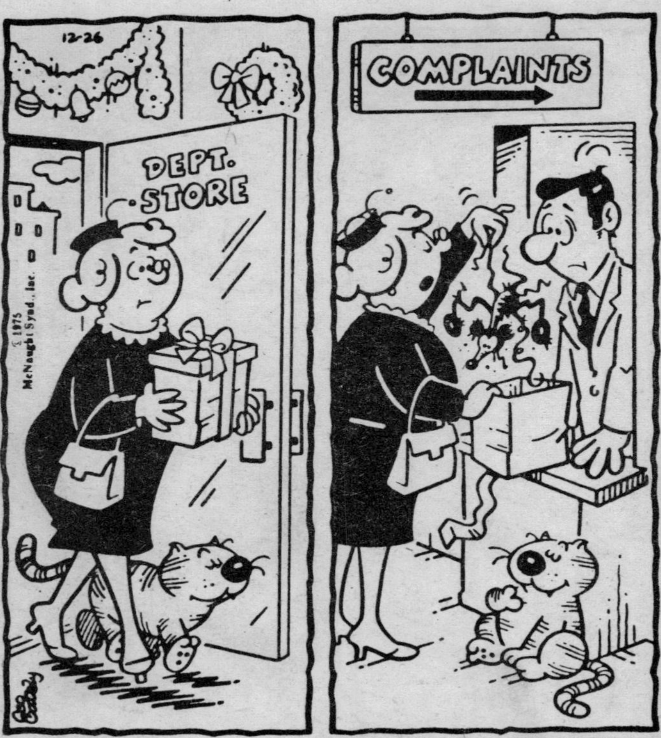
12-26
DEPT. STORE
© 1975 McNaught Synd., Inc.
COMPLAINTS

"ABOUT THIS GUARANTEED INDESTRUCTIBLE CAT TOY..."

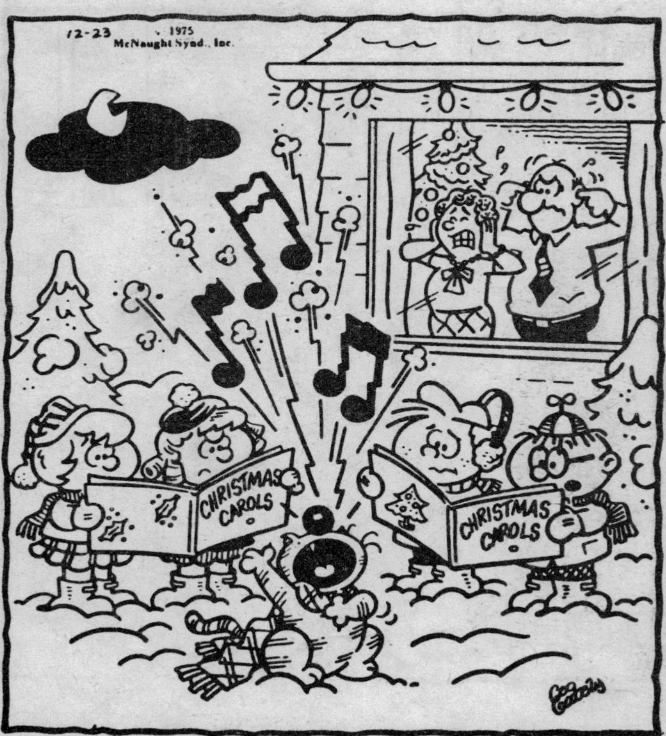
12-23 © 1975 McNaught Synd., Inc.
CHRISTMAS CAROLS
CHRISTMAS CAROLS

"DID YOU HAVE TO BRING ***HIM*** ALONG?"

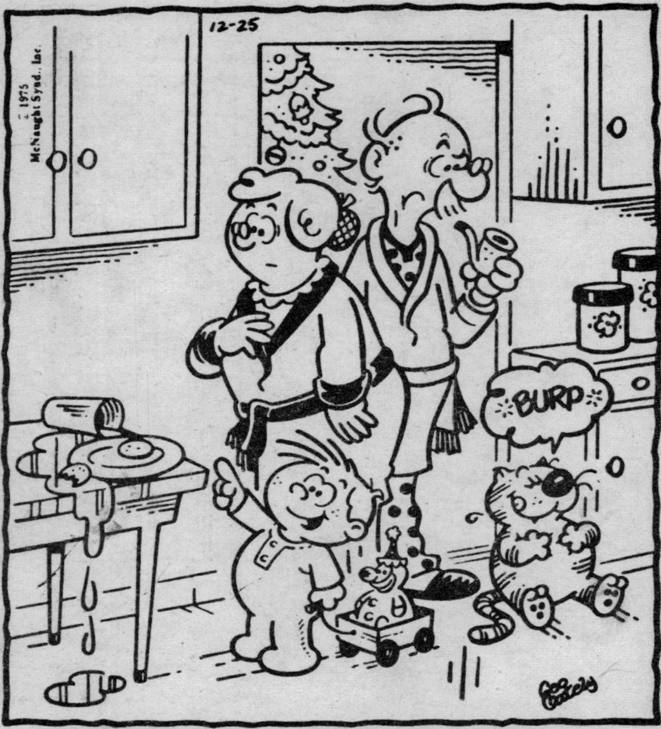
12-25
© 1975 McNaught Synd., Inc.
BURP

"LOOK, GRANDMA!-SANTA ATE UP ALL THE COOKIES AND MILK WE LEPT HIM!"

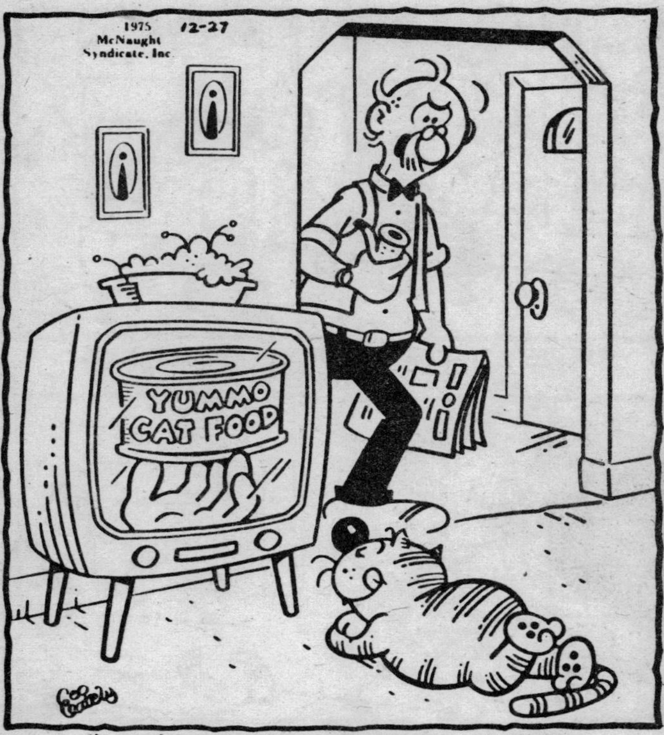
1975
McNaught
Syndicate, Inc.
12-27
YUMMO
CAT FOOD

"YOU'RE BEING PUNISHED!... I SAID 'NO TELEVISION FOR A WEEK!'"

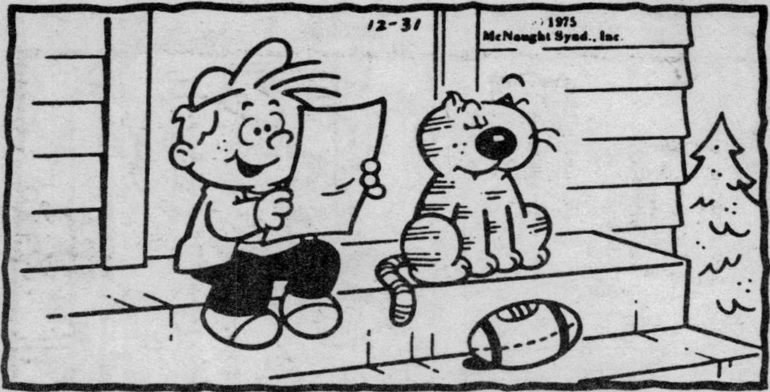
12-31
©1975 McNaught Synd., Inc.

"HERE'S A LIST OF NEW YEAR'S RESOLUTIONS I MADE FOR YOU, HEATHCLIFF..."

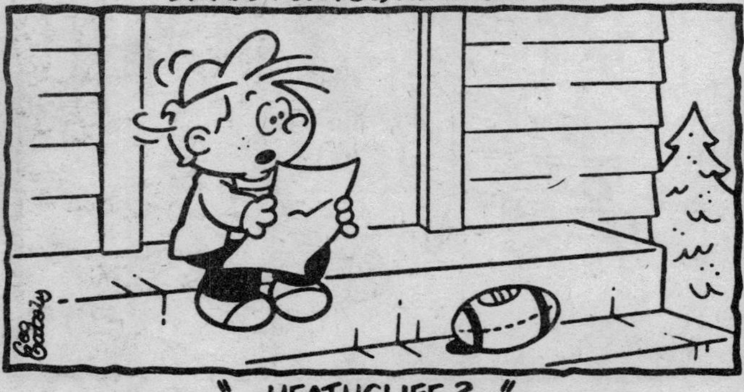

"...HEATHCLIFF ?..."

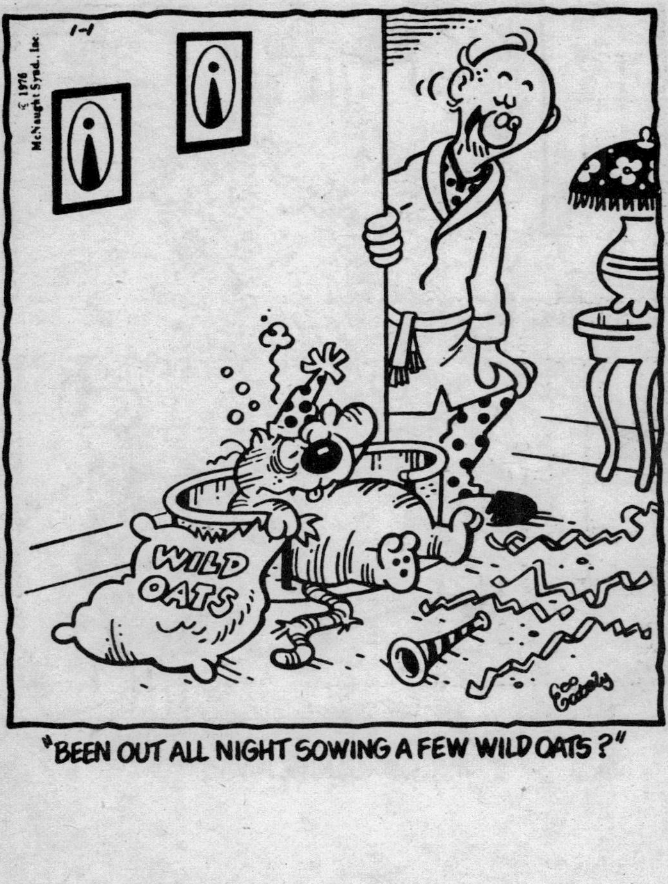
© 1978 McNaught Synd., Inc.
1-1
WILD OATS

"BEEN OUT ALL NIGHT SOWING A FEW WILD OATS?"

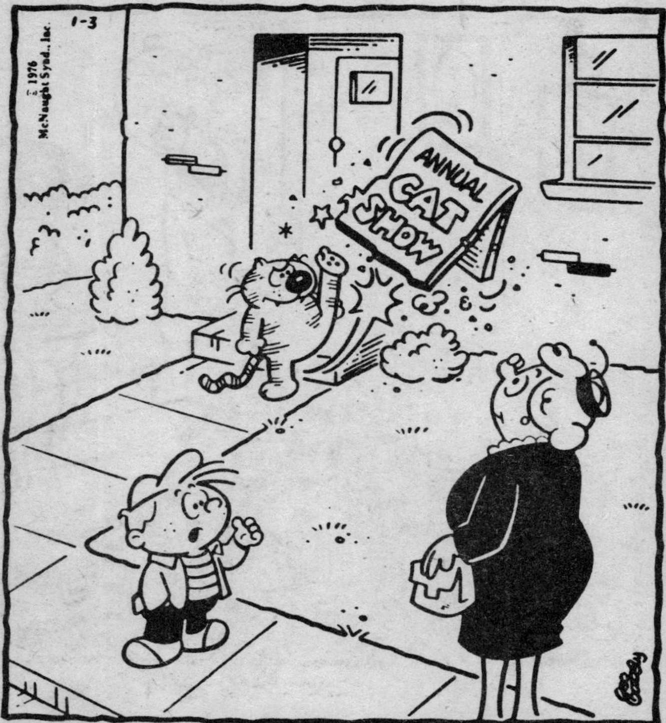
1-3
© 1976 McNaught Synd., Inc.
ANNUAL
CAT
SHOW

"HE DIDN'T WIN, BUT THEY VOTED HIM 'MR. CONGENIALITY'."

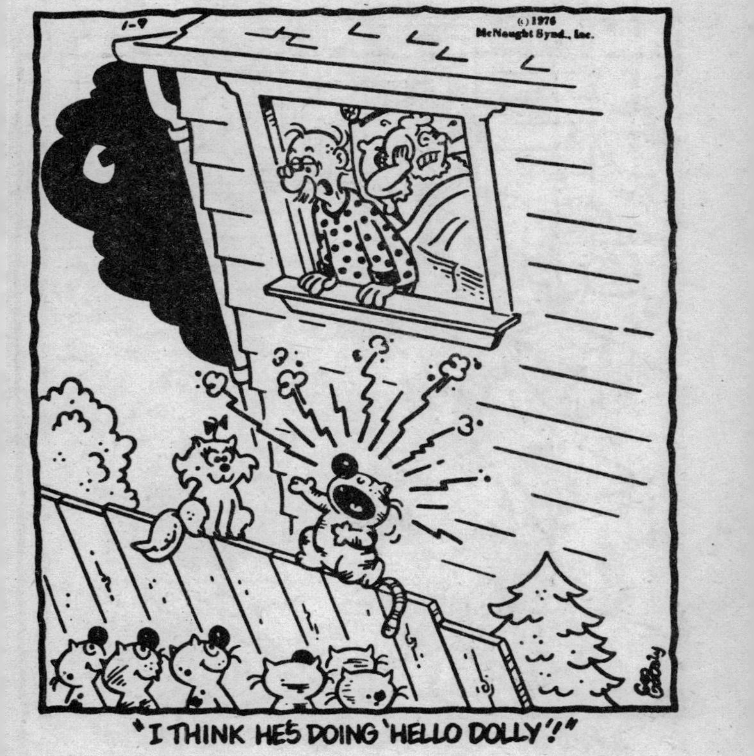
1-9
(c) 1976
McNaught Synd., Inc.

"I THINK HE'S DOING 'HELLO DOLLY'!"

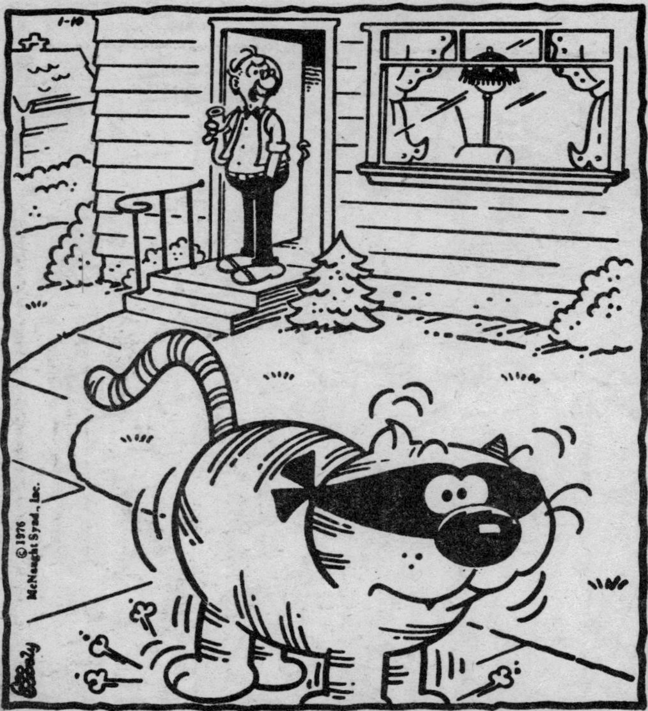
1-10
© 1976
McNaught Synd., Inc.

"...AND STAY AWAY FROM THAT FISH MARKET!"

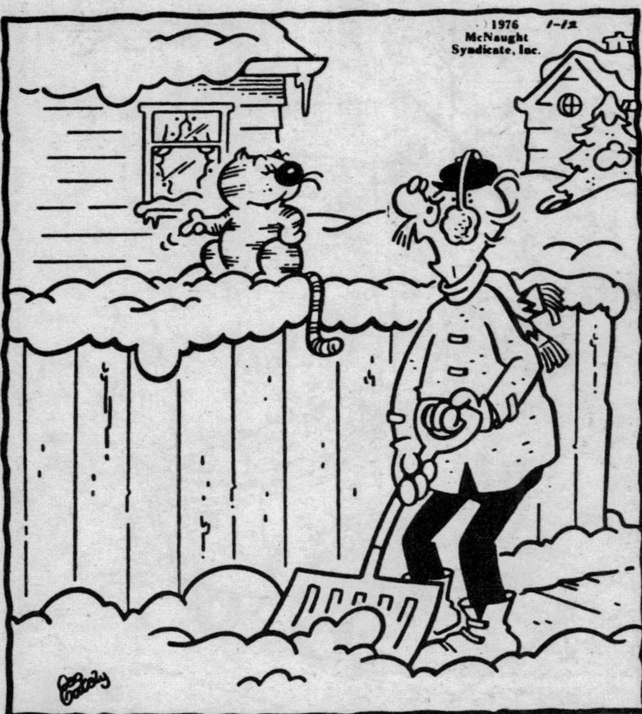

© 1976 McNaught Syndicate, Inc.
1-12

"NO!...I'M ***NOT*** GOING TO SHOVEL THE FENCE!"

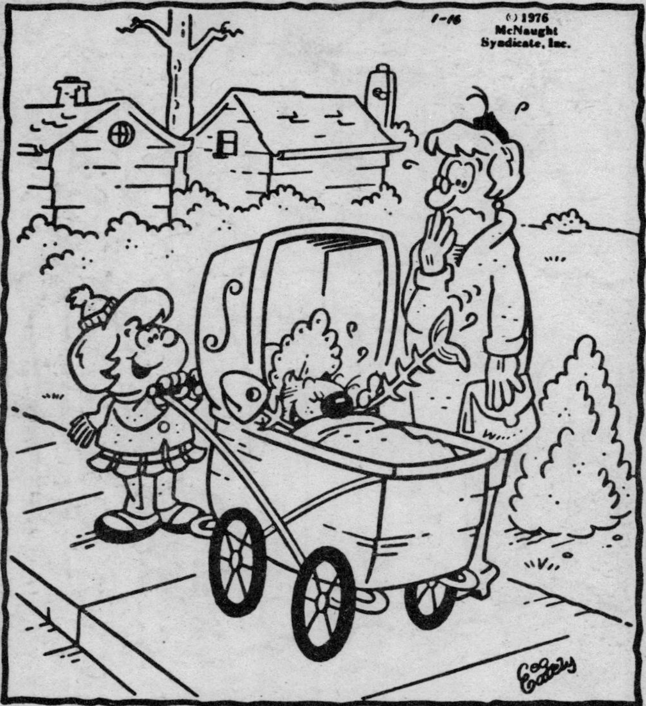
1-16
© 1976
McNaught
Syndicate, Inc.

"BABY IS TEETHING."

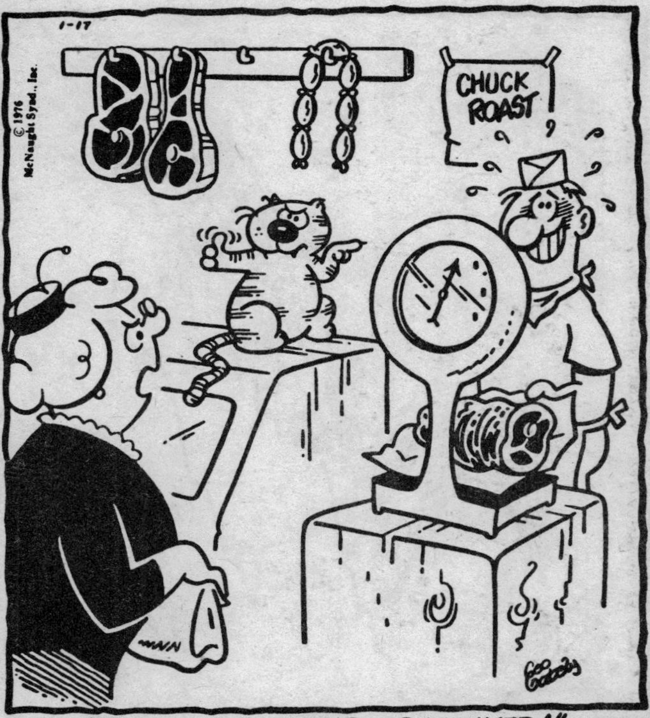
1-17
© 1976 McNaught Synd., Inc.
CHUCK ROAST

"WATCH YOUR THUMB, MR. KLINKER!"

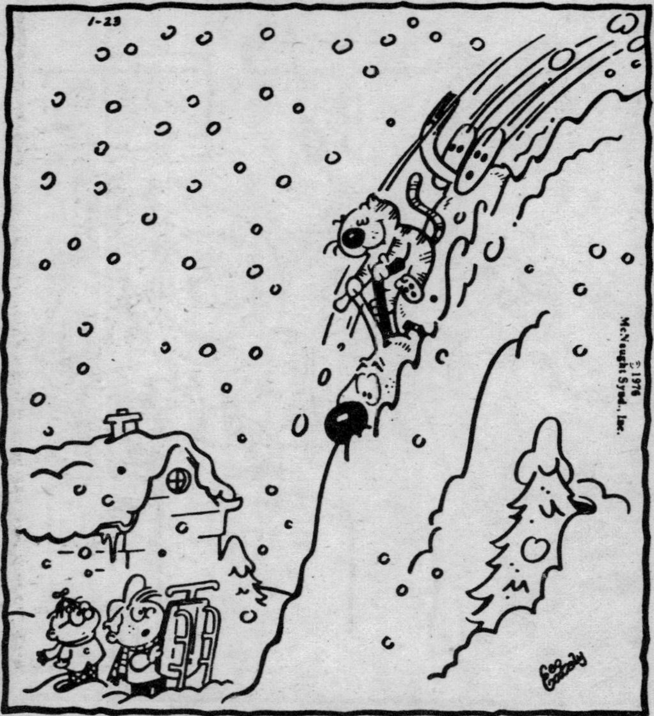
1-23
©1976 McNaught Synd., Inc.
Geo Gately

"HERE COMES HEATHCLIFF WITH HIS SLED DOG!"

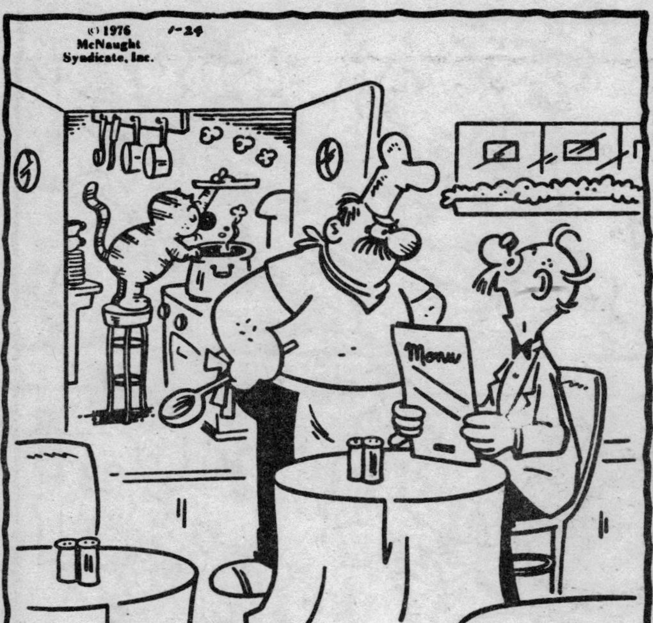

© 1976 McNaught Syndicate, Inc.
1-24
Menu

"WHY, NO...I DIDN'T SEND ANYONE IN TO INSPECT THE KITCHEN!"

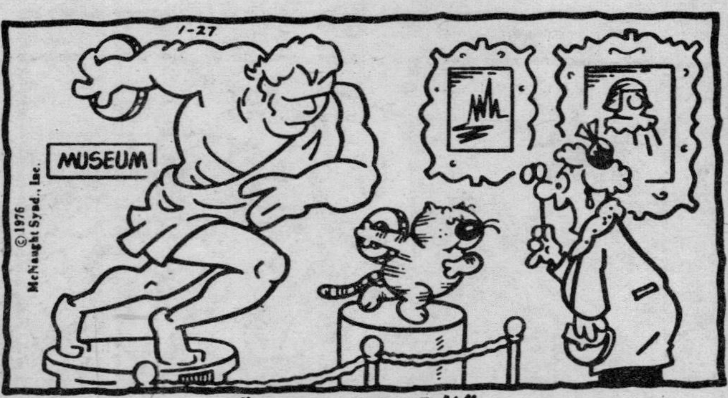
1-27
MUSEUM
© 1976 McNaught Synd., Inc.

"MARVELOUS!!"

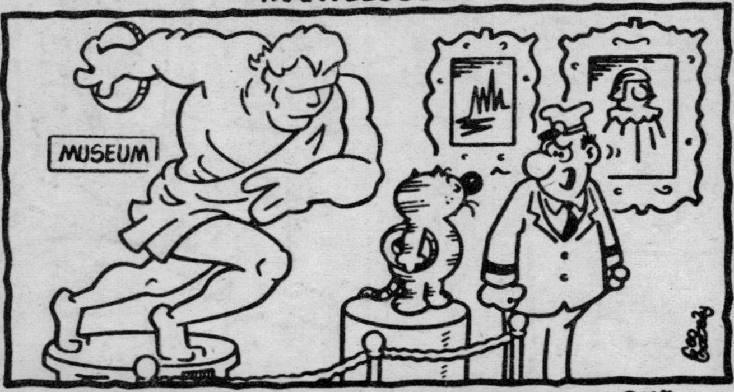
MUSEUM

"WILL YOU TAKE YOUR DISH AND GO HOME?!!"

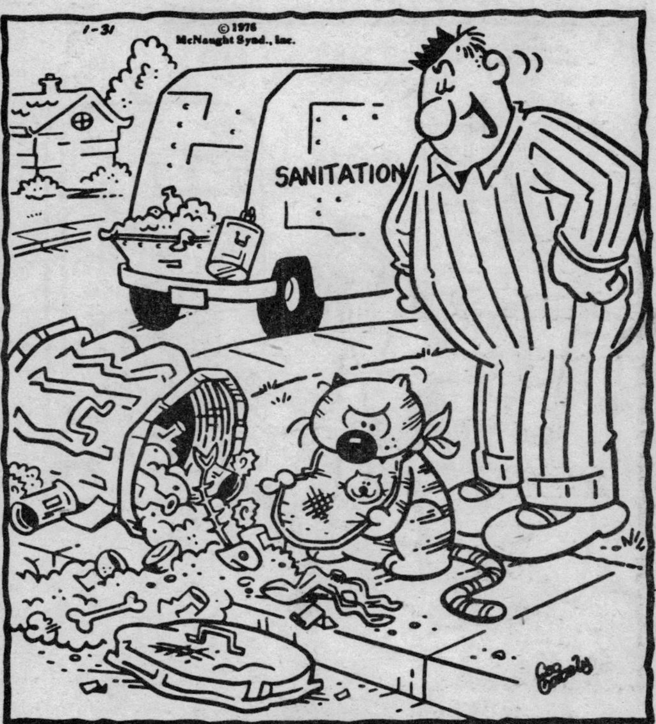
1-31
© 1976
McNaught Synd., Inc.
SANITATION

"STAIN YOUR BIB?"

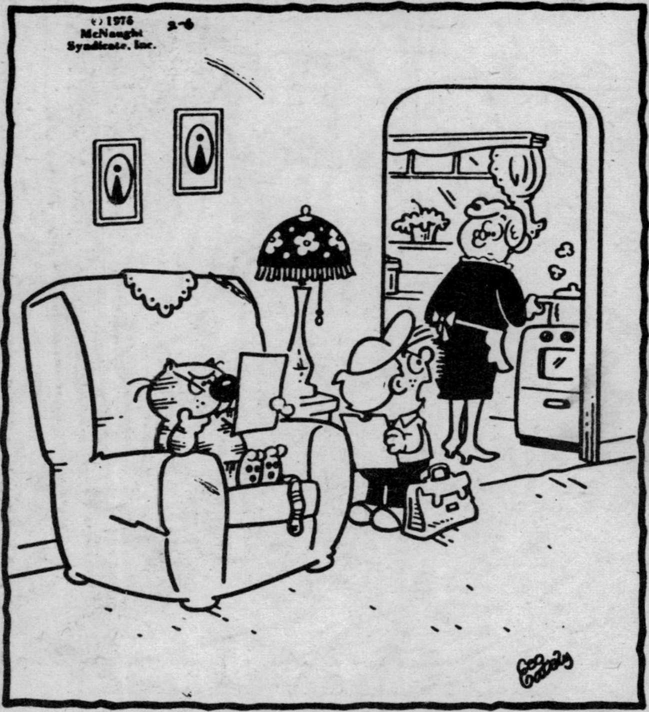

© 1976
McNaught
Syndicate, Inc.
2-6

"WE GOT OUR REPORT CARDS TODAY...
HEATHCLIFF IS LOOKING AT IT."

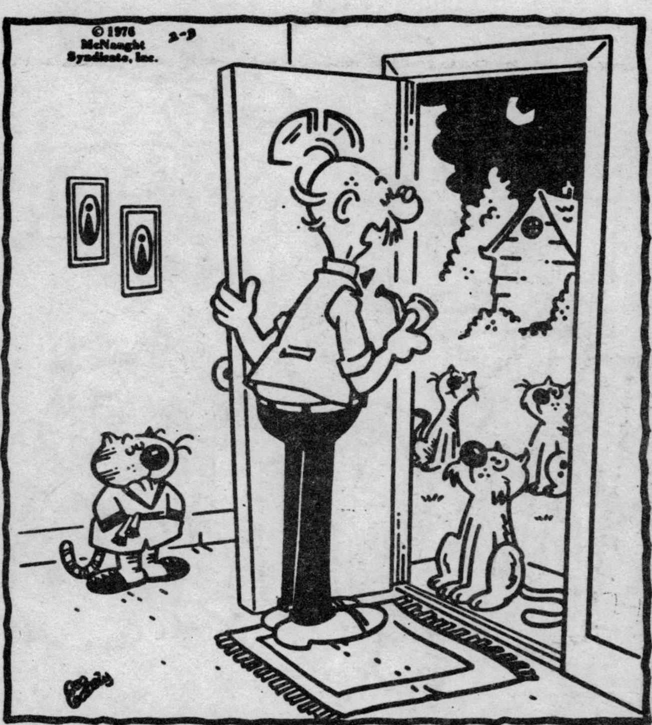
© 1976
McNaught
Syndicate, Inc.
2-9

"HEATHCLIFF'S NOT GOING OUT TONIGHT."

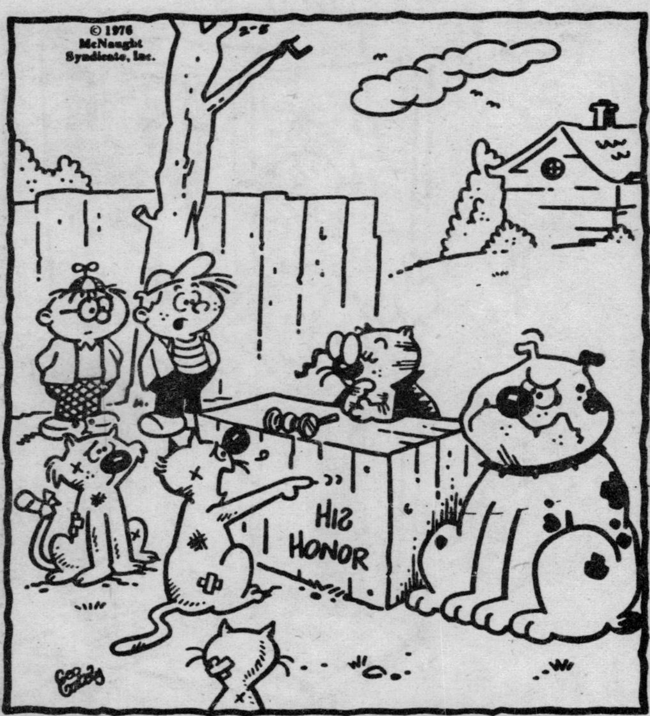
© 1976 McNaught Syndicate, Inc.
2-5
HIS HONOR

"HEATHCLIFF IS HOLDING HEARINGS CONCERNING SPIKE'S BEHAVIOR."

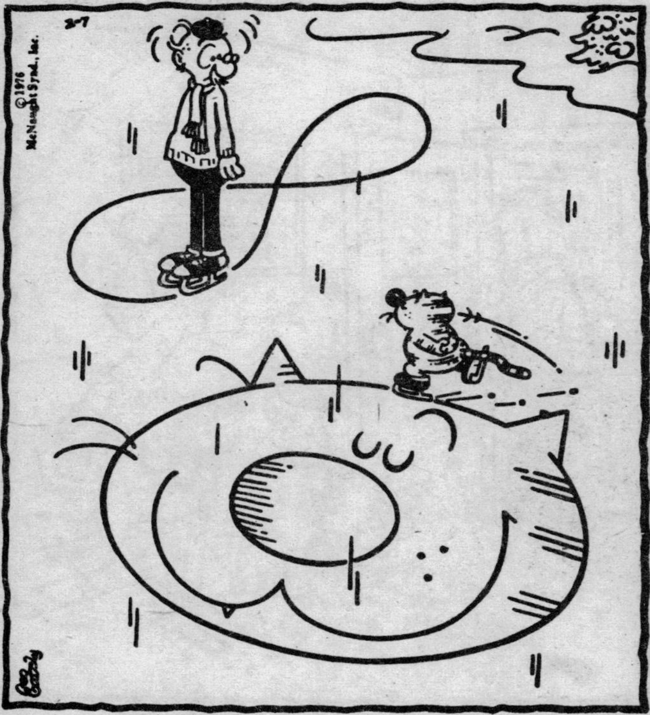
©1976
McNaught Synd., Inc.
2-7

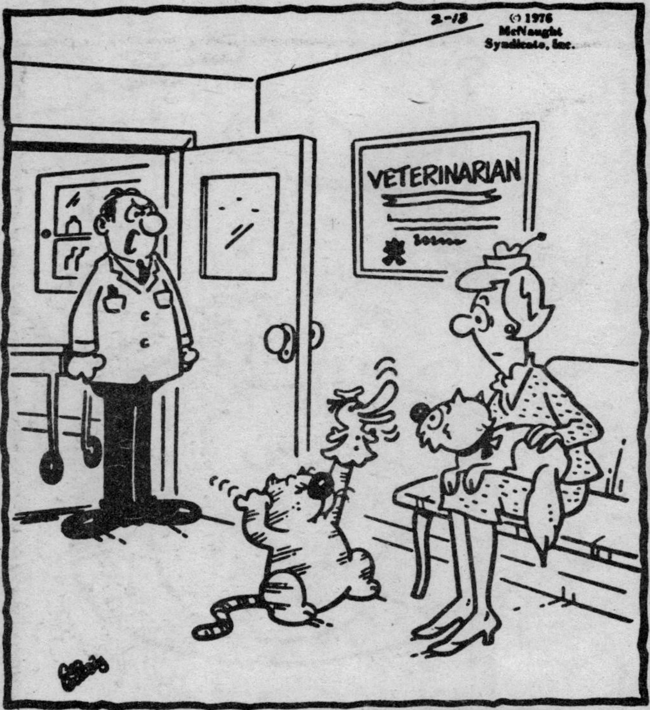
2-13
© 1976
McNaught
Syndicate, Inc.
VETERINARIAN

"WHO ARE YOU CALLING A QUACK ?!"

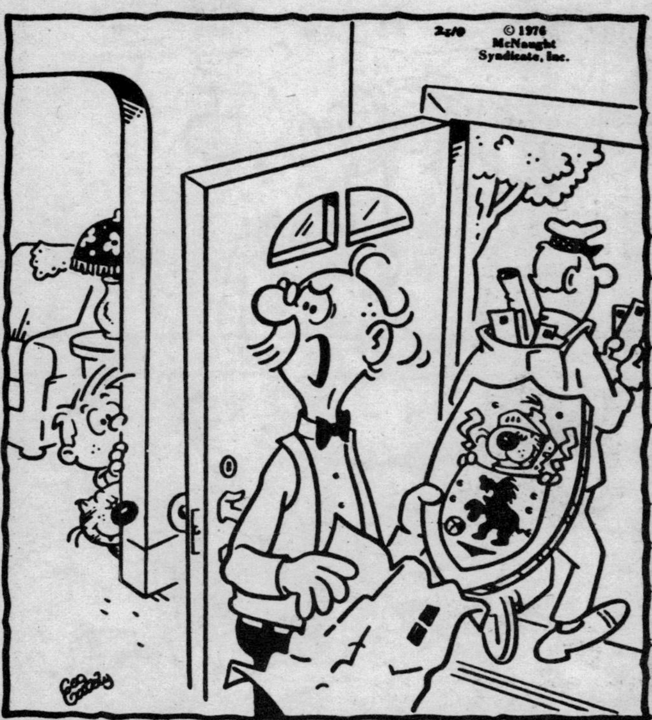

2-10
© 1976 McNaught Syndicate, Inc.

"WHO SPENT $7.98 ON HEATHCLIFF'S COAT OF ARMS?!"

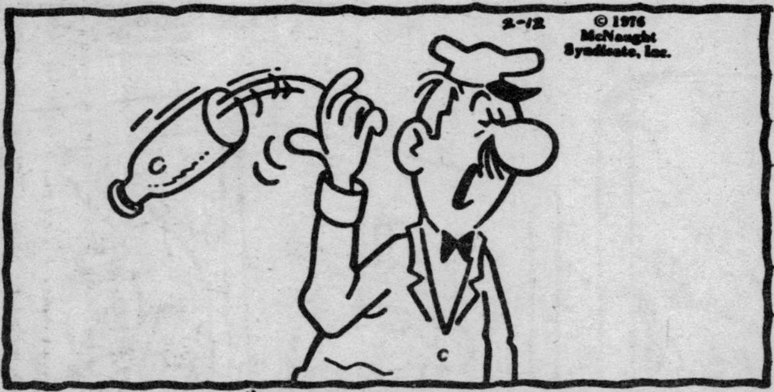
2-12
© 1976
McNaught
Syndicate, Inc.

"WHAT THE HECK!...

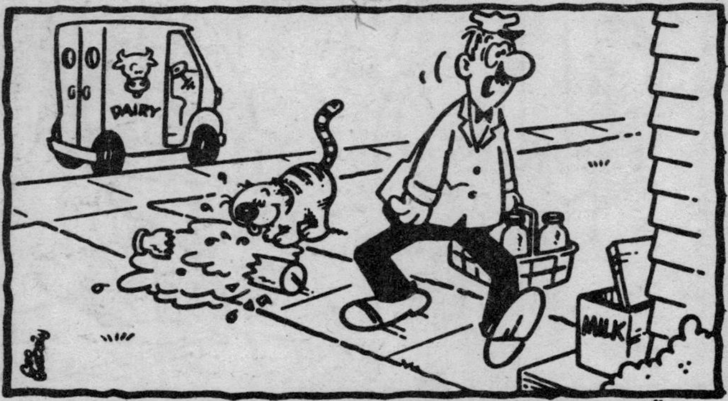
DAIRY
MILK

...HE'LL ONLY MAKE ME BREAK ONE ANYWAY!"

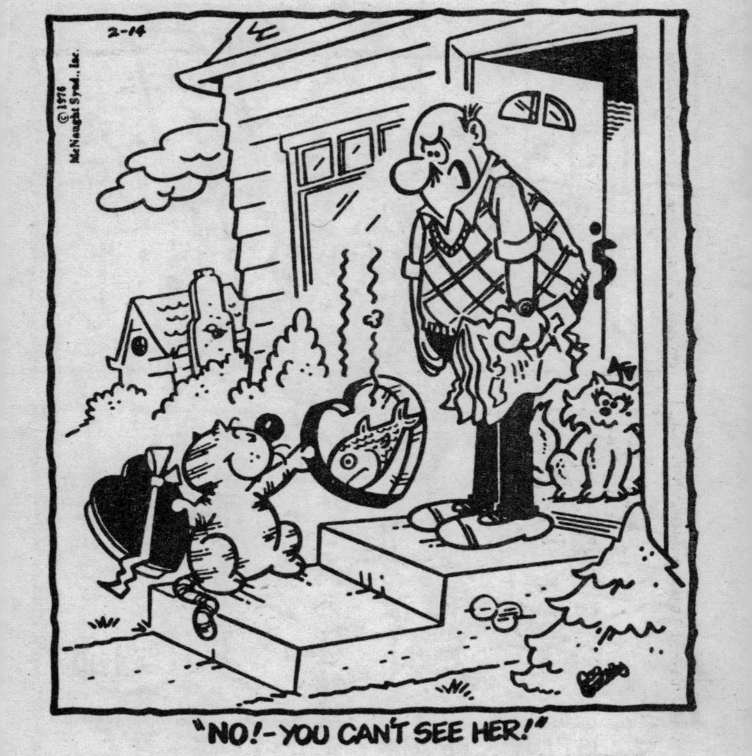
2-14
©1976 McNaught Synd., Inc.

"NO!-YOU CAN'T SEE HER!"

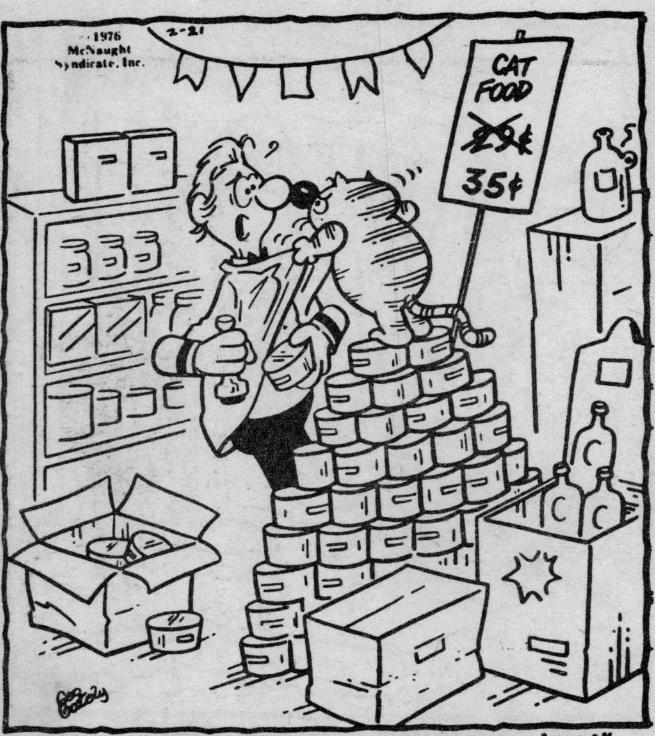
© 1976
McNaught
Syndicate, Inc.
2-21
CAT
FOOD
29¢
35¢

"I JUST MARK 'EM THE WAY THEY PRICE 'EM!"

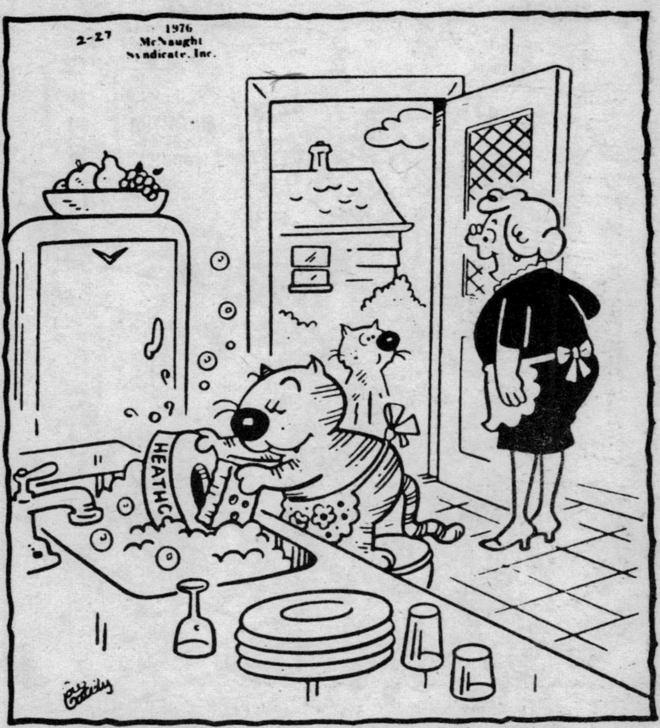
2-27
1976
McNaught
Syndicate, Inc.
HEATHC

"HE'LL BE OUT SOON... HE'S DOING HIS DISH."

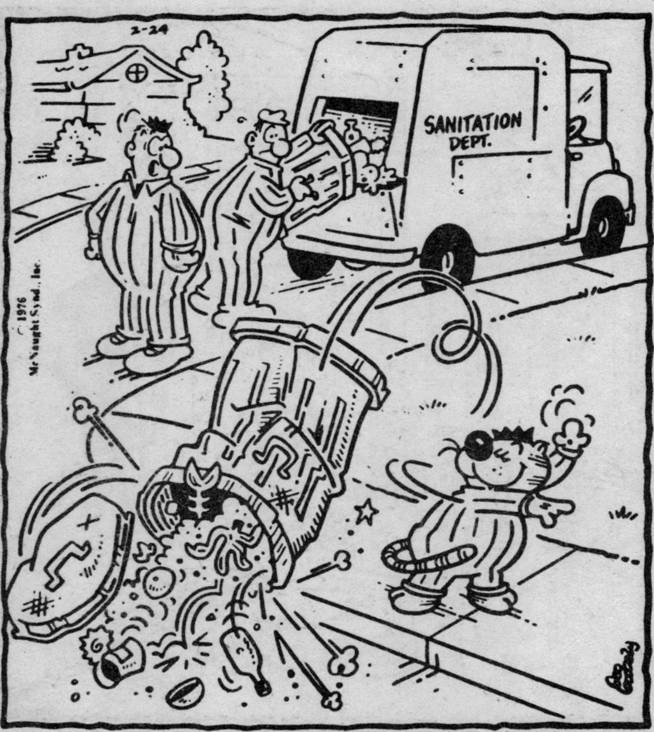
2-24
SANITATION
DEPT.
© 1976 McNaught Synd., Inc.

"WILL YOU LOOK AT THAT!...NOW HE'S EVEN GOT HIS OWN UNIFORM!"

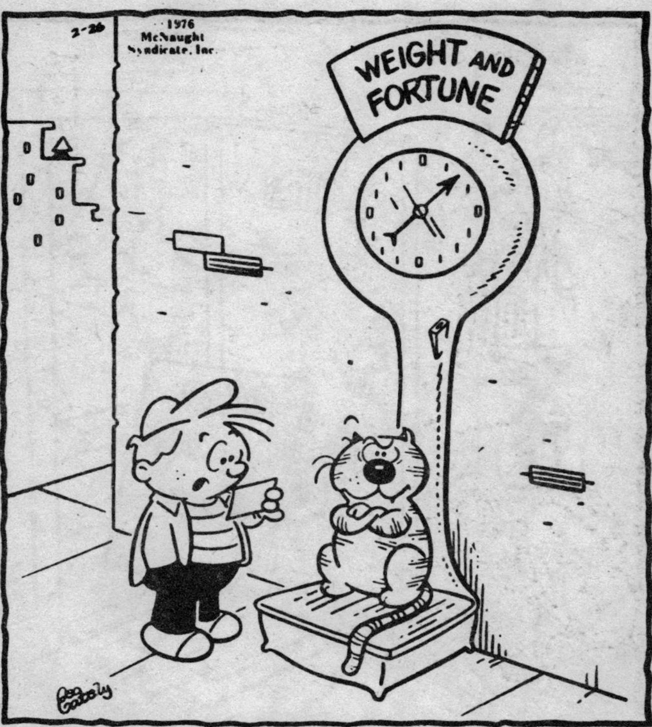

2-26
©1976 McNaught Syndicate, Inc.
WEIGHT AND FORTUNE

"YOU'RE A CONNIVING CUSS WHO IS EIGHT POUNDS OVERWEIGHT!"

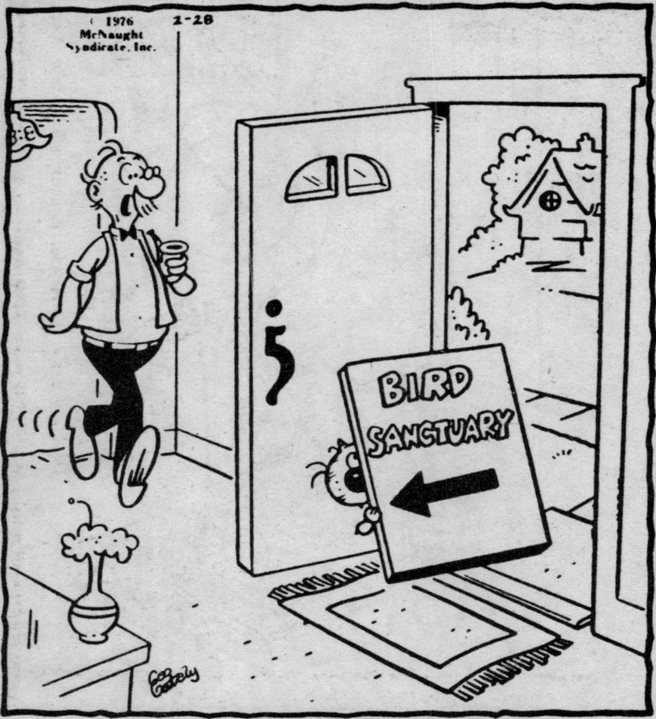
© 1976 McNaught Syndicate, Inc.
2-28
BIRD SANCTUARY

"NOW, WHO LEFT THAT DOOR OPEN?!"

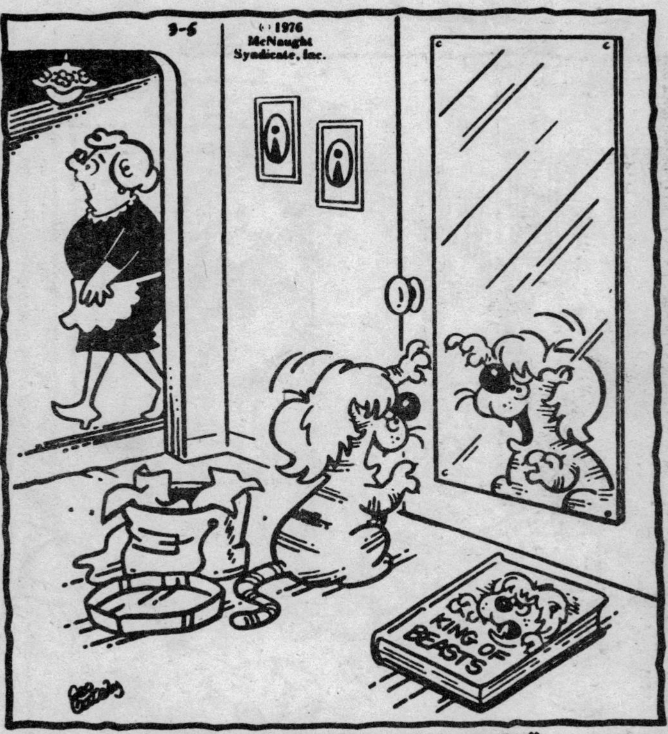
3-6
© 1976
McNaught
Syndicate, Inc.
KING OF
BEASTS

"HAS ANYONE SEEN MY WIG ?!"

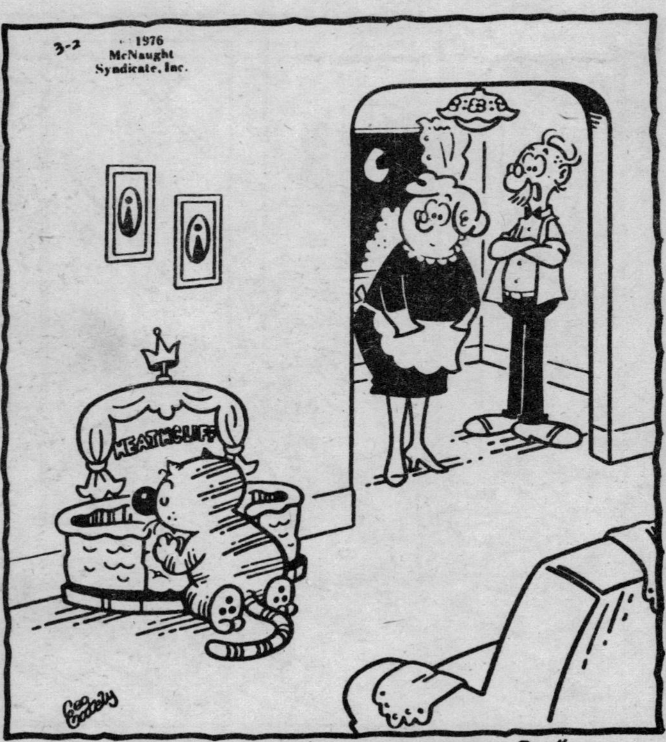
3-2
© 1976
McNaught
Syndicate, Inc.
HEATHCLIFF

"OH, OH!...WHAT'S HE DONE NOW?!!"

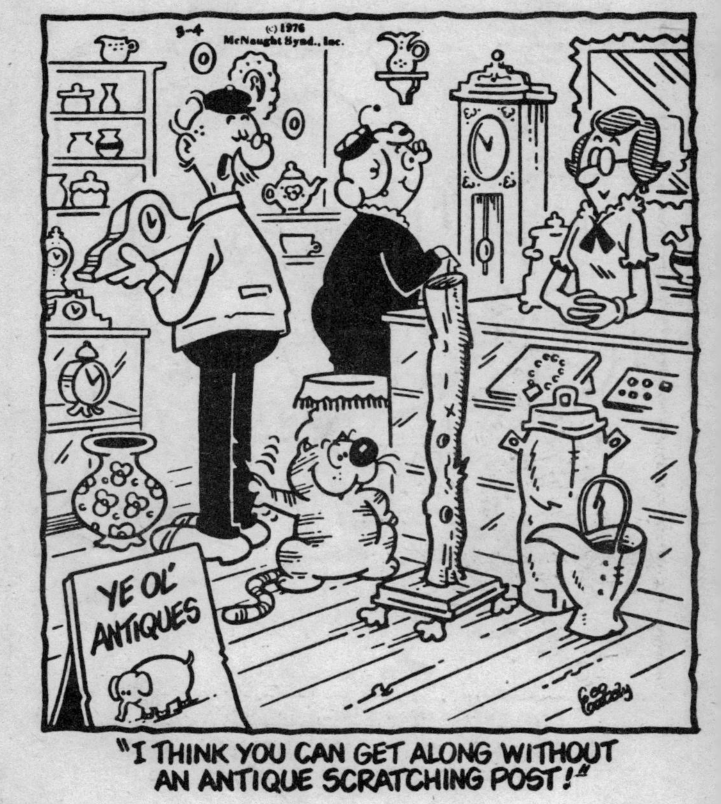

8-4
(c) 1976
McNaught Synd., Inc.
YE OL'
ANTIQUES

"I THINK YOU CAN GET ALONG WITHOUT AN ANTIQUE SCRATCHING POST!"

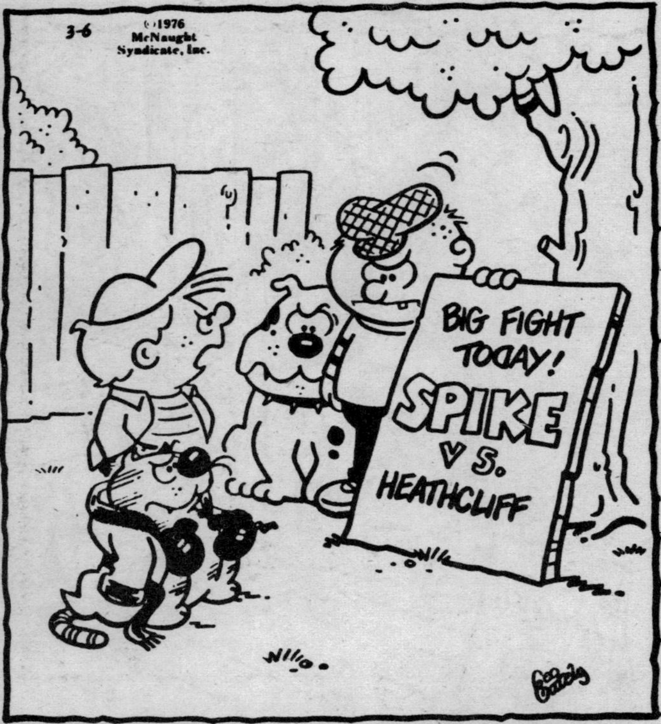
3-6
©1976
McNaught
Syndicate, Inc.
BIG FIGHT
TODAY!
SPIKE
VS.
HEATHCLIFF

"THE FIGHT'S OFF!... HEATHCLIFF NEVER
TAKES SECOND BILLING!"

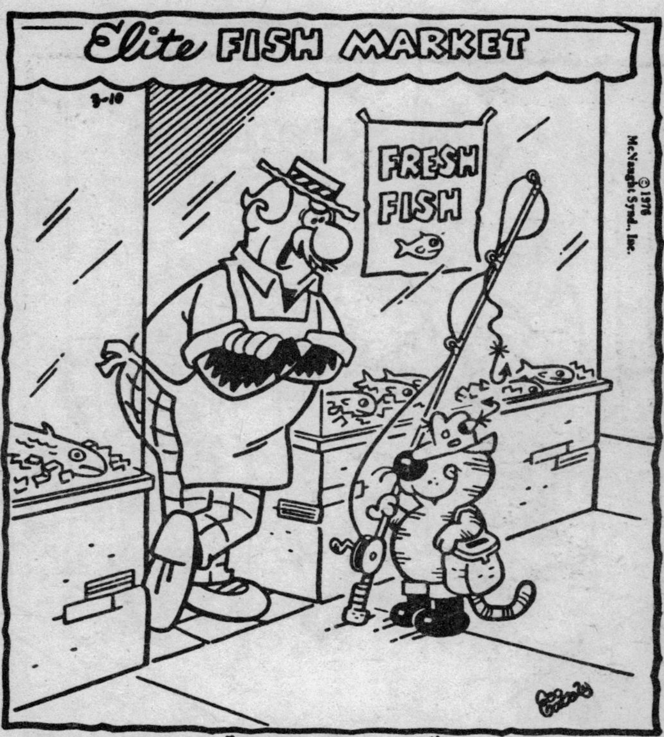
Elite FISH MARKET
3-10
FRESH
FISH
© 1976
McNaught Synd., Inc.

"GET LOST!"

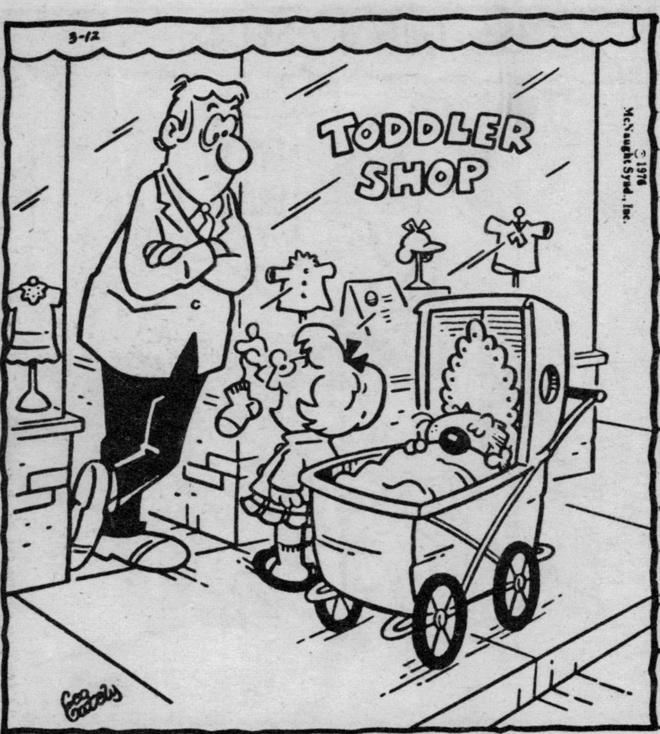
3-12
TODDLER SHOP
© 1978 McNaught Synd., Inc.

"CAN YOU BRONZE A CAT BOOTY?"

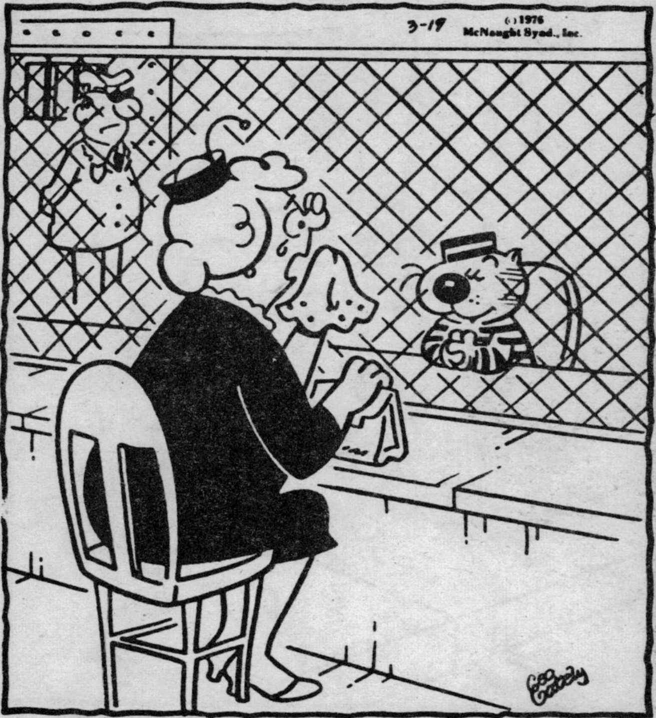
3-19
(c) 1976
McNaught Synd., Inc.

"DON'T WORRY, DEAR...WE'LL GET YOU A GOOD LAWYER."

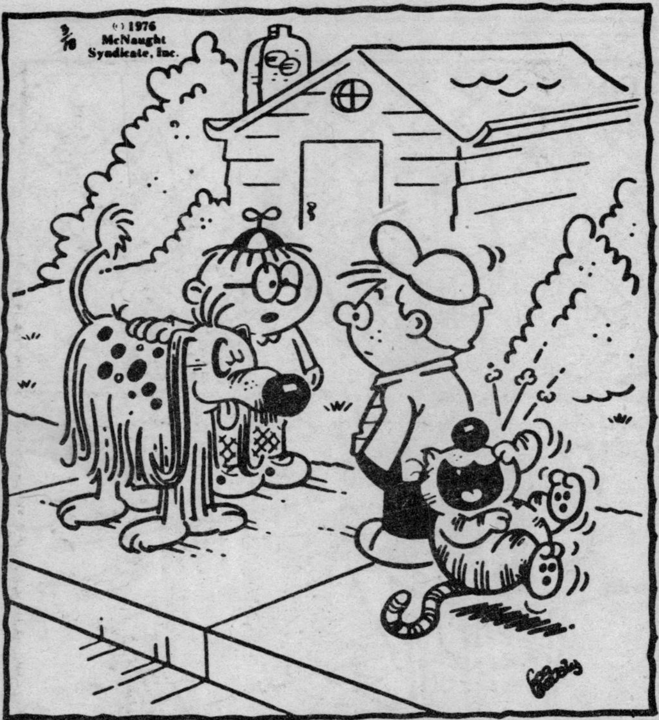
3/18
© 1976
McNaught
Syndicate, Inc.

"HE'S A MIXED BREED."

"DON'T GRAB FOR THINGS AT THE TABLE, SPIKE!"

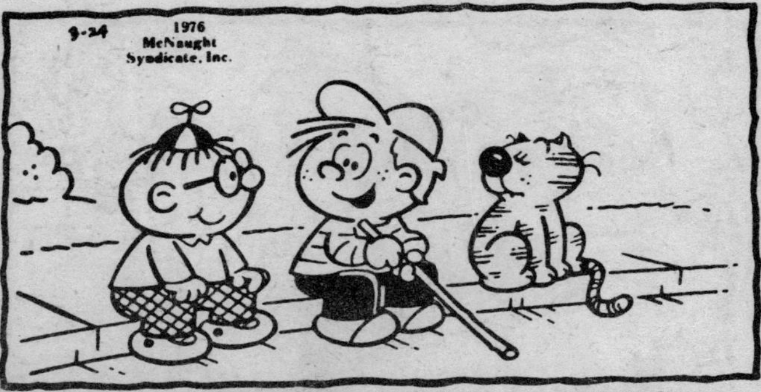
8-24
1976
McNaught
Syndicate, Inc.

"YEAH, THE YANKS LOOK GOOD THIS YEAR, AND THE PIRATES...

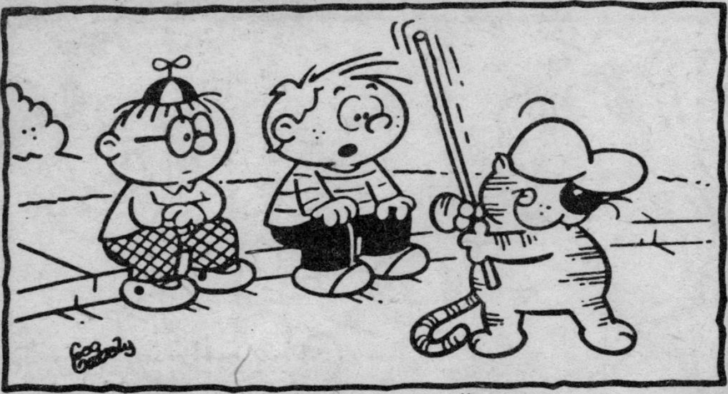

...AND THE TIGERS!"

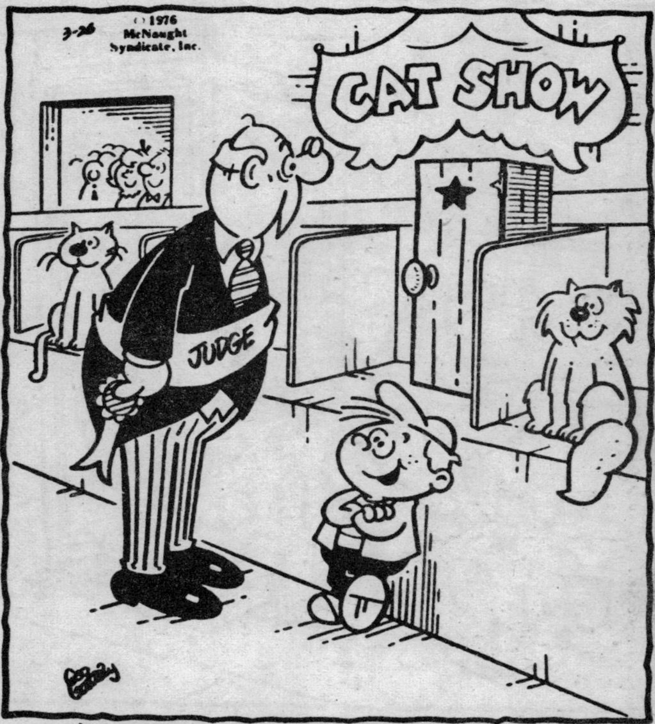
3-26
© 1976 McNaught Syndicate, Inc.
CAT SHOW
JUDGE

"HEATHCLIFF IS IN HIS DRESSING ROOM."

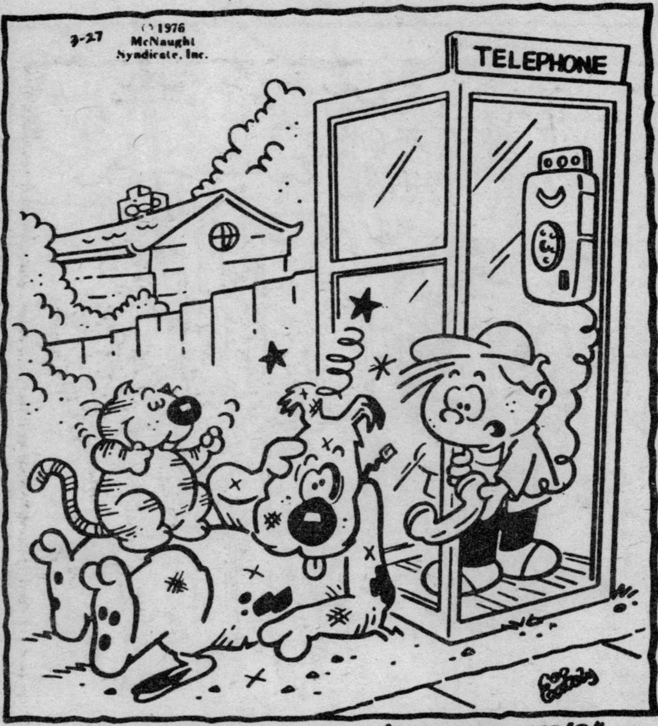
3-27
© 1976
McNaught
Syndicate, Inc.
TELEPHONE

"WOULD YOU LIKE TO TALK TO 'DIAL A PRAYER'?"

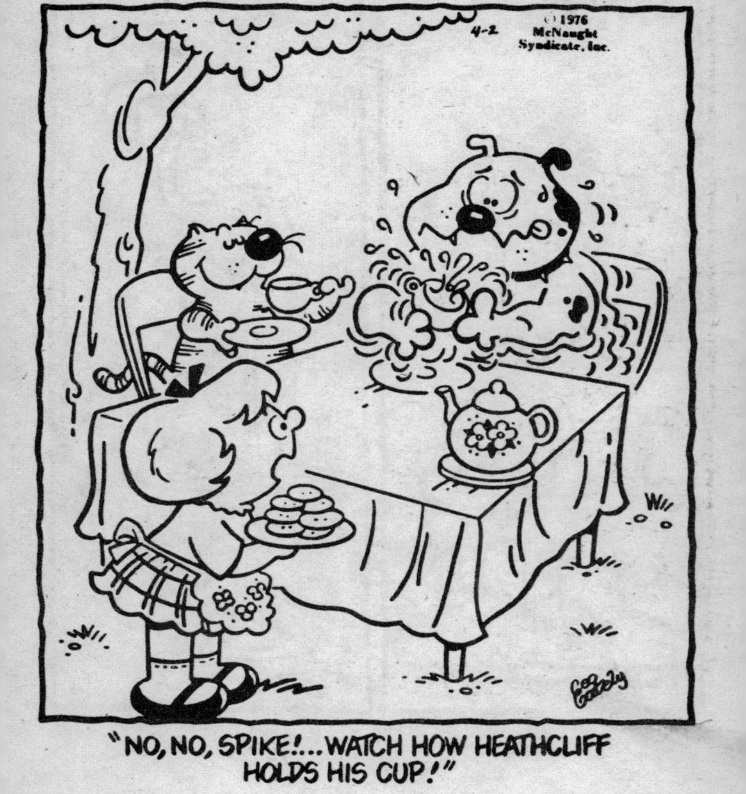
4-2
© 1976
McNaught
Syndicate, Inc.

"NO, NO, SPIKE!...WATCH HOW HEATHCLIFF HOLDS HIS CUP!"

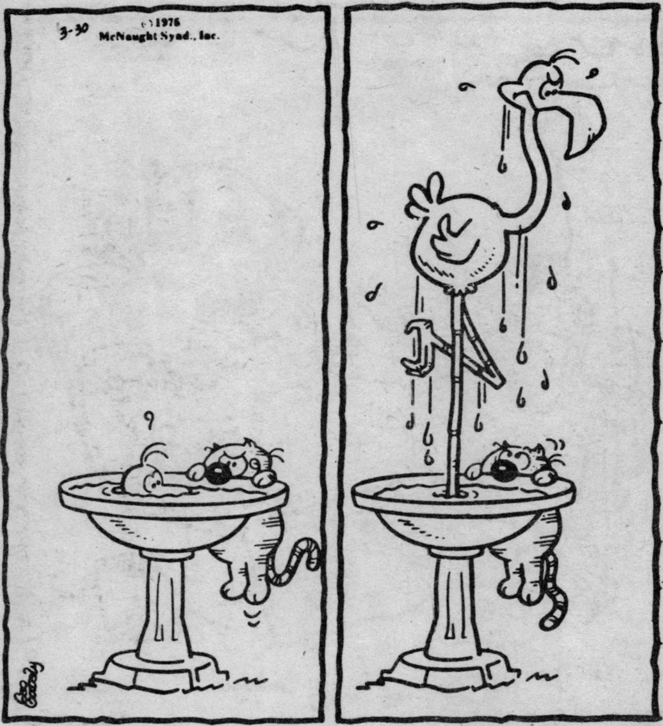
3-30
© 1976
McNaught Synd., Inc.

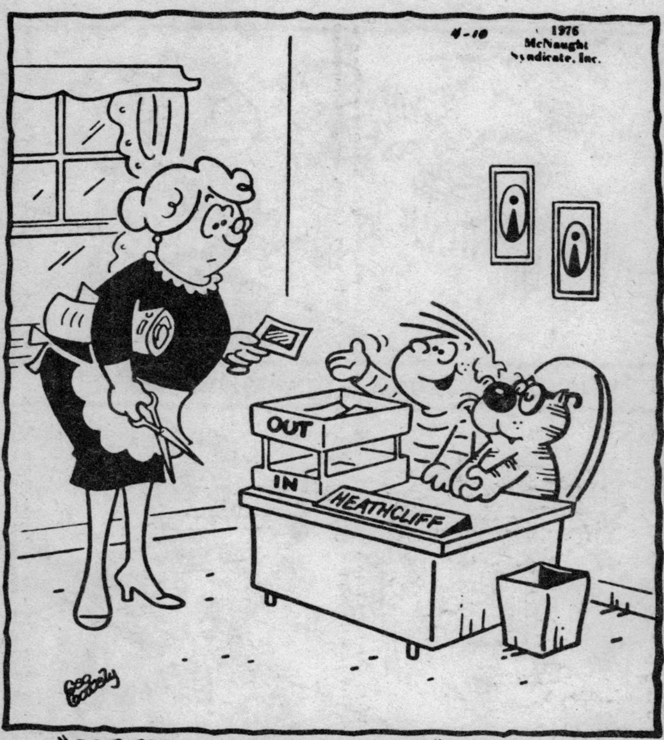
4-10
1976
McNaught
Syndicate, Inc.
OUT
IN
HEATHCLIFF

"CAT FOOD COUPONS GO IN THE "IN" BASKET."

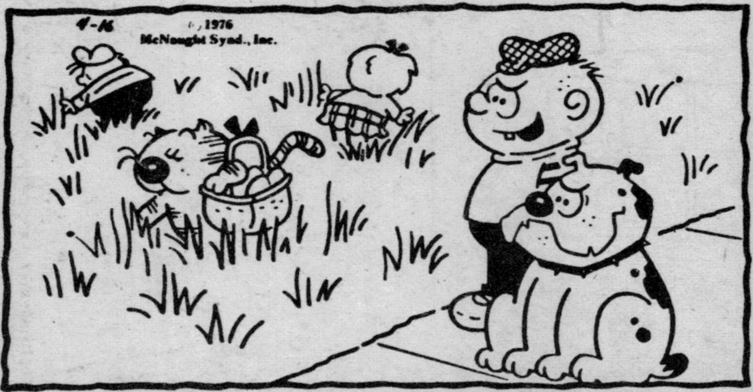
4-16
© 1976
McNaught Synd., Inc.

"WELL, AIN'T THAT CUTE!...LOOK WHO'S HUNTING EASTER...

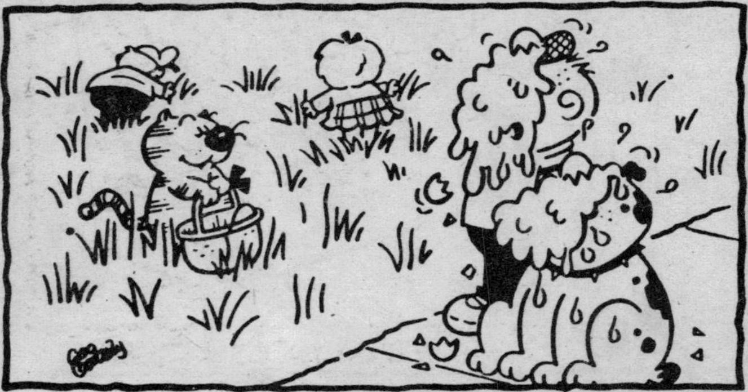

...EGGS!"

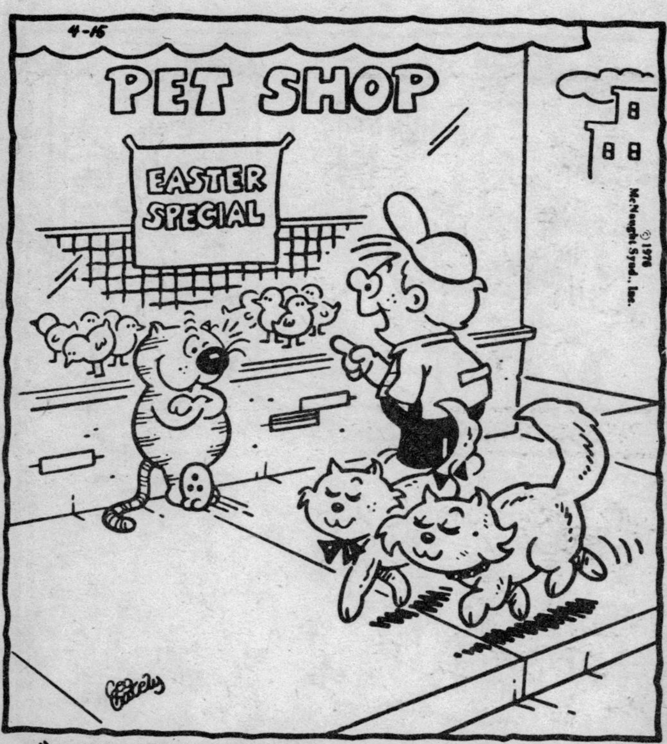
4-15
PET SHOP
EASTER SPECIAL
© 1976 McNaught Synd., Inc.

"LOOK, HEATHCLIFF!...LOOK AT THE CUTE CHICKS!"

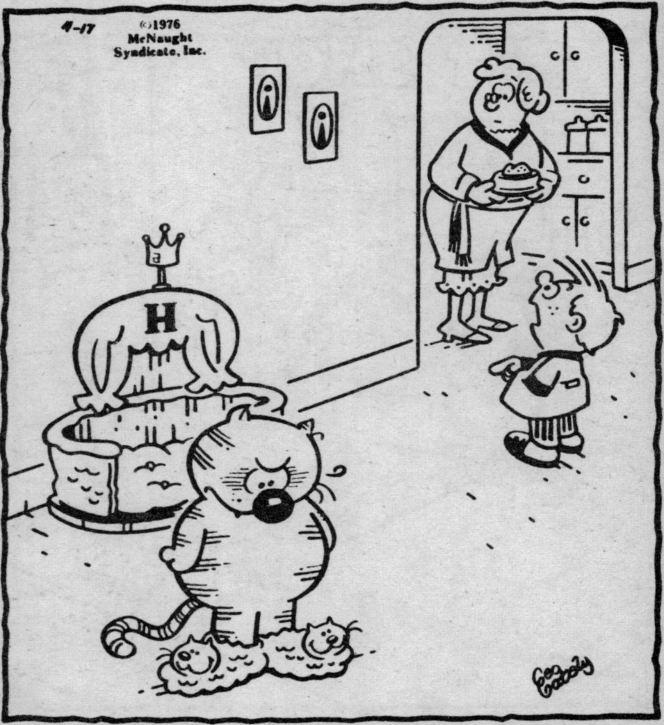

4-17
©1976
McNaught
Syndicate, Inc.
H

"HE'S EMBARRASSED...HE WON'T COME TO BREAKFAST IN HIS NEW SLIPPERS."

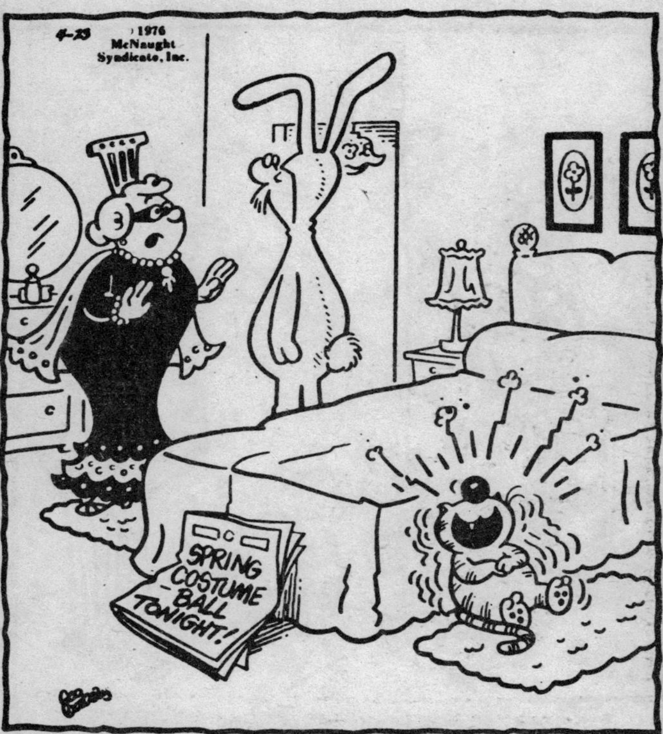
4-23
© 1976
McNaught
Syndicate, Inc.
SPRING
COSTUME
BALL
TONIGHT!

"NEVER MIND HEATHCLIFF...I THINK YOU LOOK FINE!"

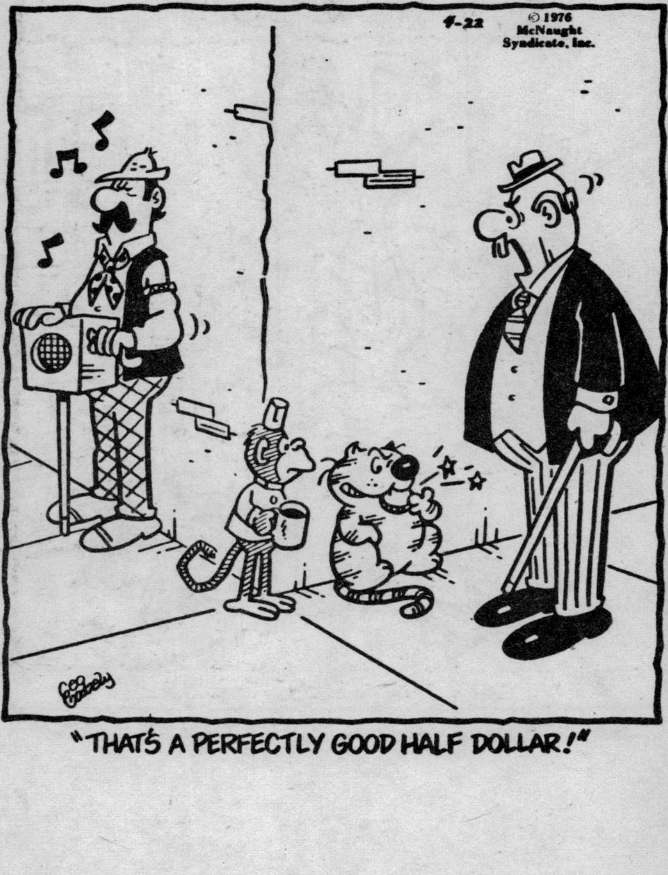
4-22
© 1976
McNaught
Syndicate, Inc.

"THAT'S A PERFECTLY GOOD HALF DOLLAR!"

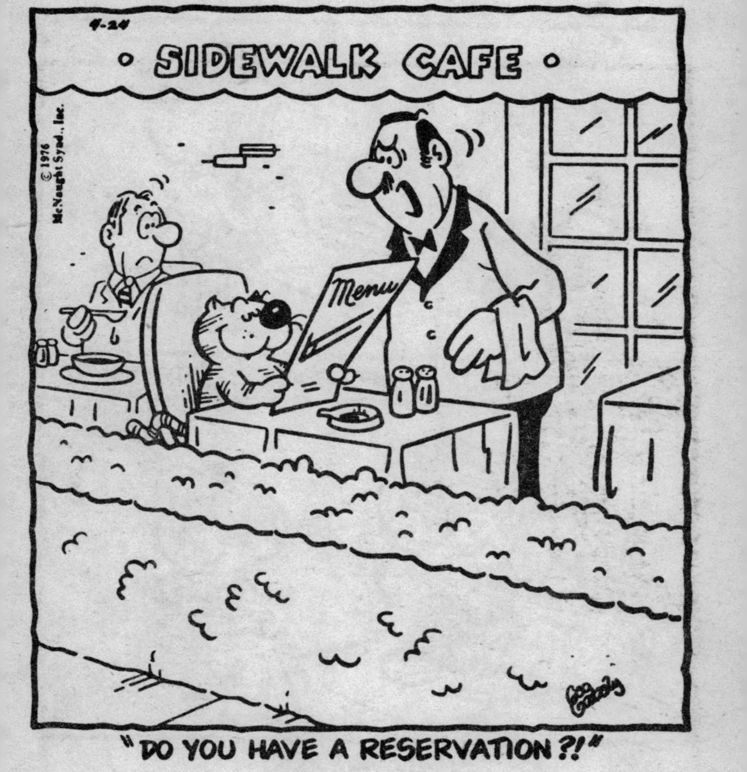
4-24
SIDEWALK CAFE
© 1976 McNaught Synd., Inc.
Menu

"DO YOU HAVE A RESERVATION?!"

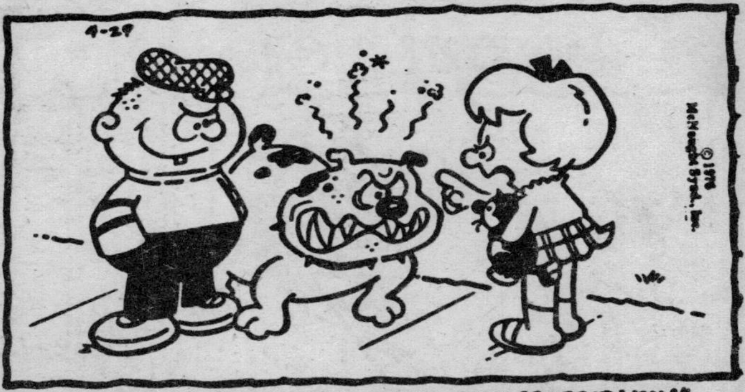
4-29

"HURT MY KITTY AND I'LL GET HEATHCLIFF AFTER YOU!"

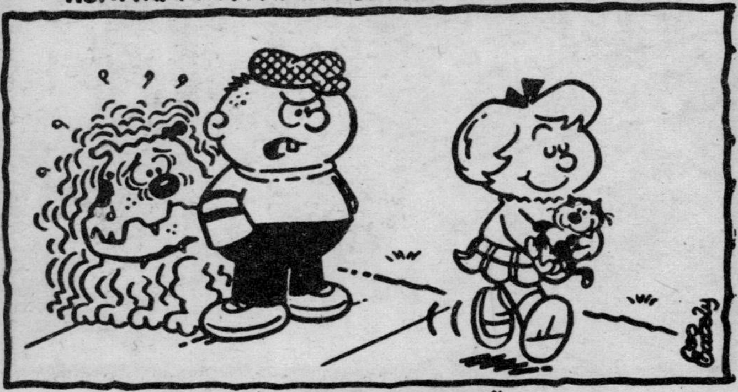

"NAMEDROPPER!"

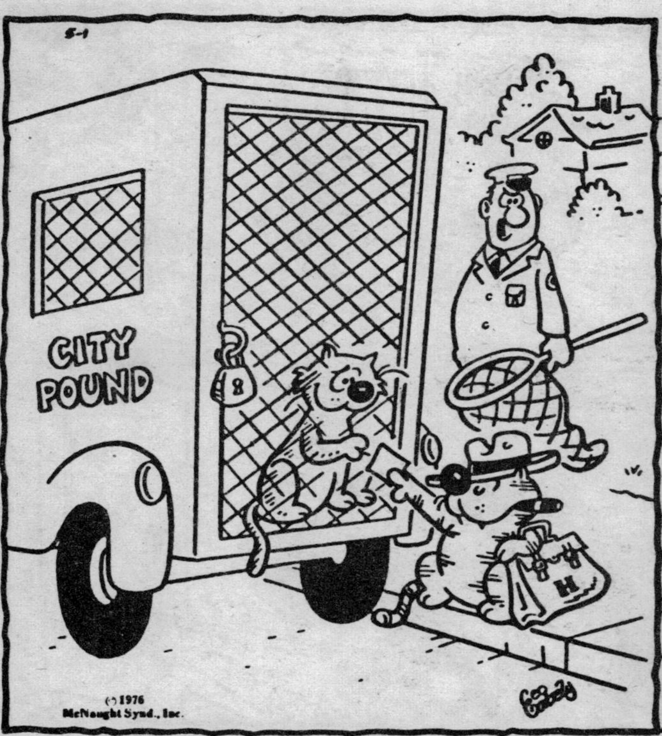
5-1
CITY POUND
(c) 1976
McNaught Synd., Inc.

"HE DOESN'T NEED A LAWYER!"

5-5
Elite FISH MARKET
© 1976 McNaught Synd., Inc.
Elite FISH MARKET

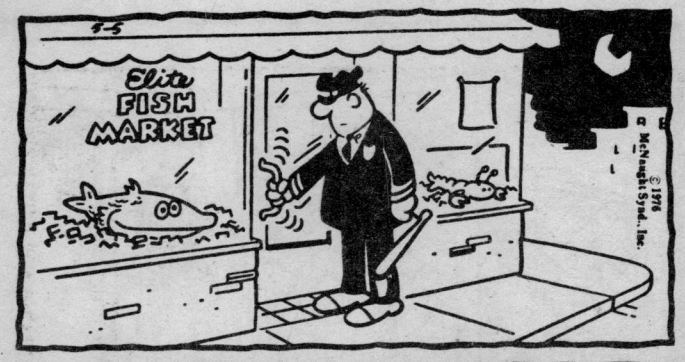

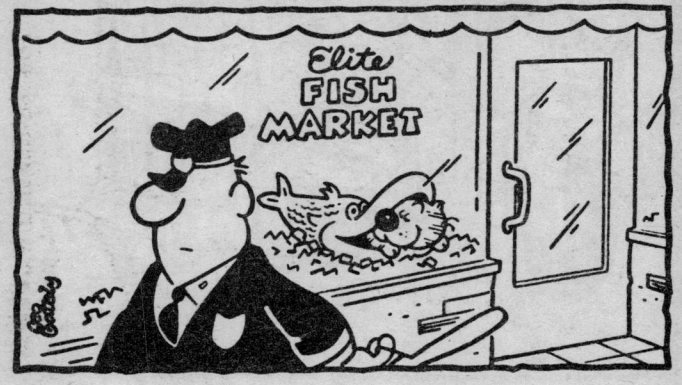

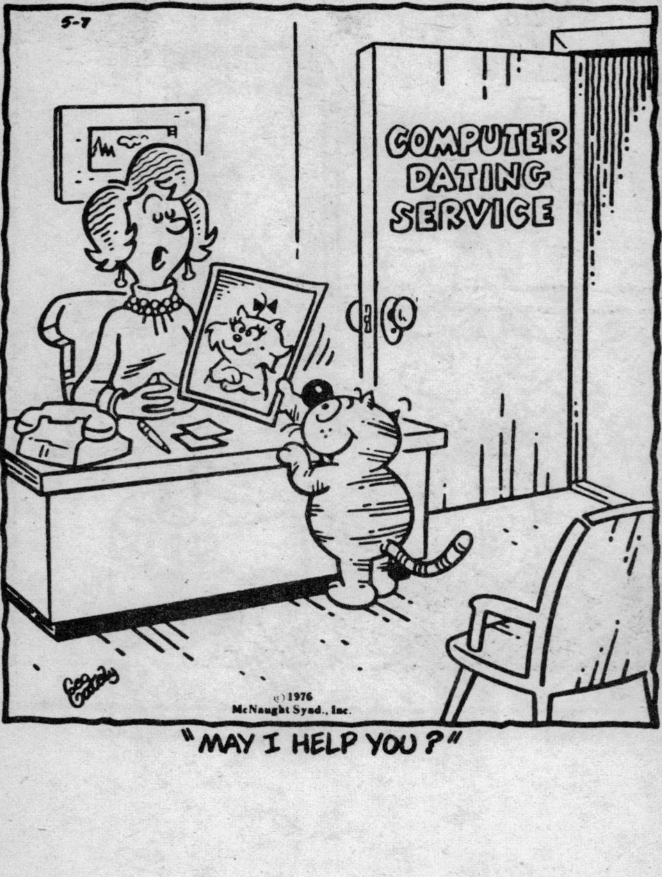
5-7
COMPUTER
DATING
SERVICE
©1976
McNaught Synd., Inc.

"MAY I HELP YOU?"

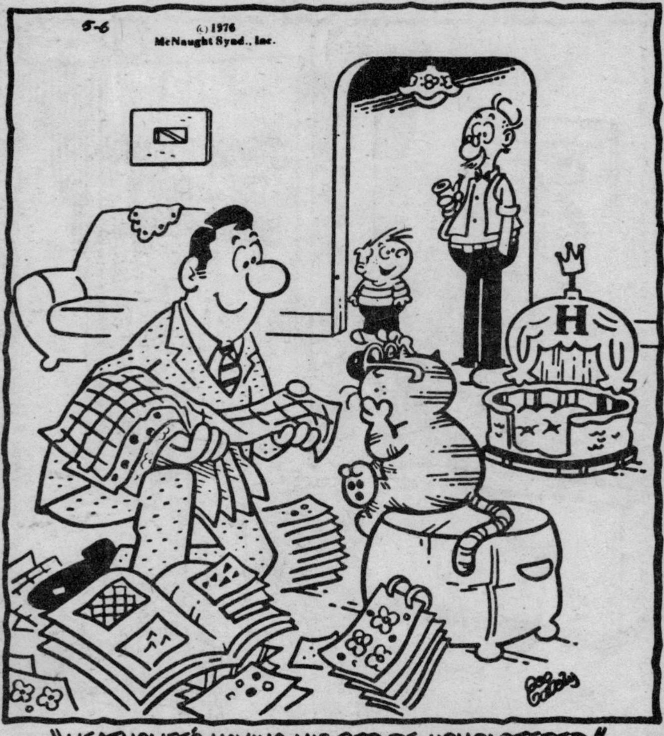
5-6
(c) 1976
McNaught Synd., Inc.
H
"HEATHCLIFF'S HAVING HIS BED RE-UPHOLSTERED."

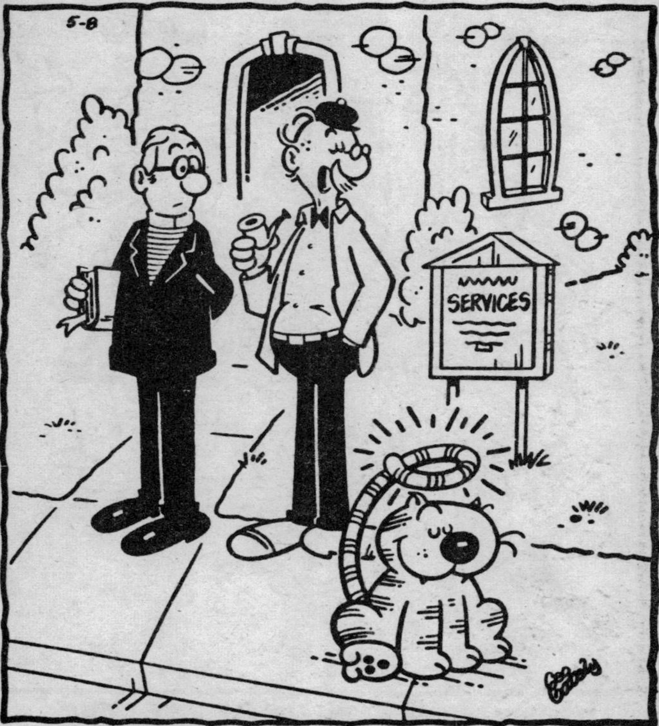
5-8
SERVICES

"I'M A BIT FED UP WITH HIS 'HOLIER THAN THOU' ATTITUDE!"

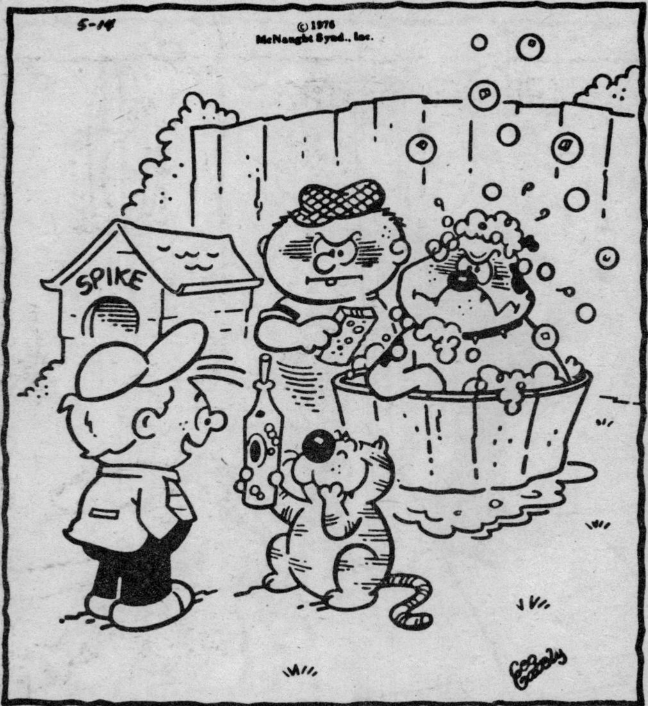
5-14
© 1976
McNaught Synd., Inc.
SPIKE

"OH, WOW!...MADEMOISELLE FIFI'S BUBBLE BATH!"

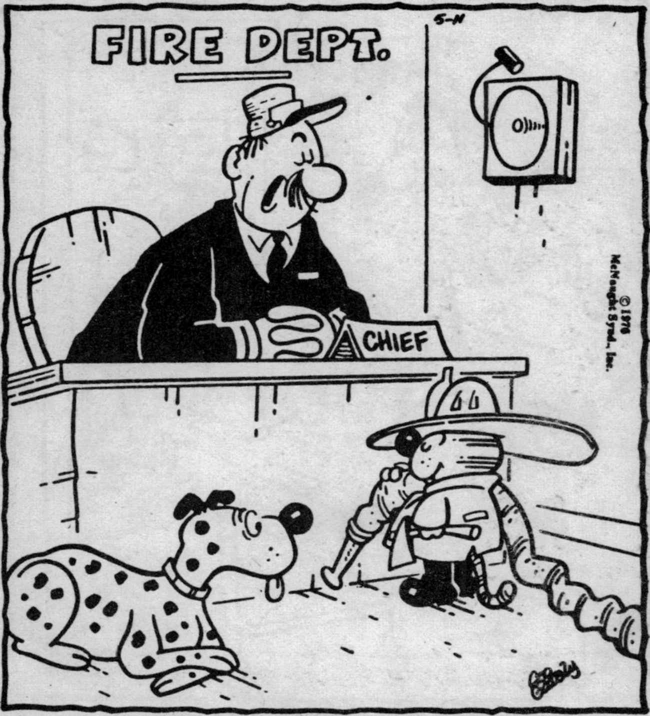
FIRE DEPT.
5-11
CHIEF
© 1978 McNaught Synd., Inc.
"WE'RE QUITE SATISFIED WITH OUR PRESENT MASCOT, THANK YOU!"

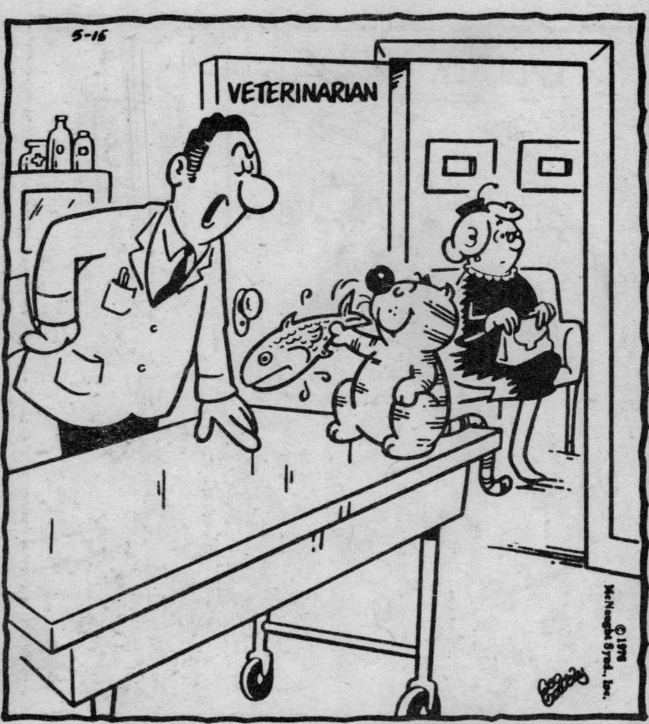
5-16
VETERINARIAN
© 1976 McNaught Synd., Inc.

"NO THANKS... YOUR OWNER CAN PAY THE BILL!"

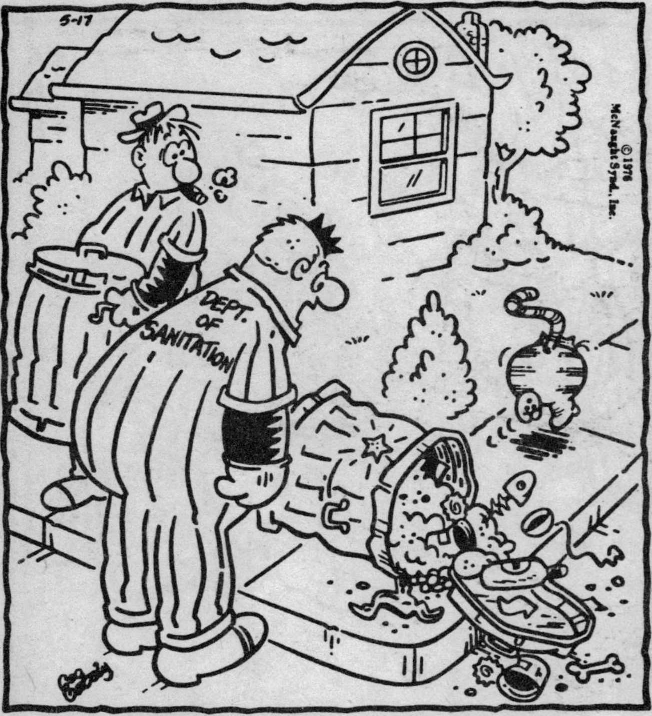
5-17
© 1976 McNaught Synd., Inc.
DEPT. OF SANITATION

"HE LIKED THIS ONE!...HE GAVE IT A GOLD STAR!"

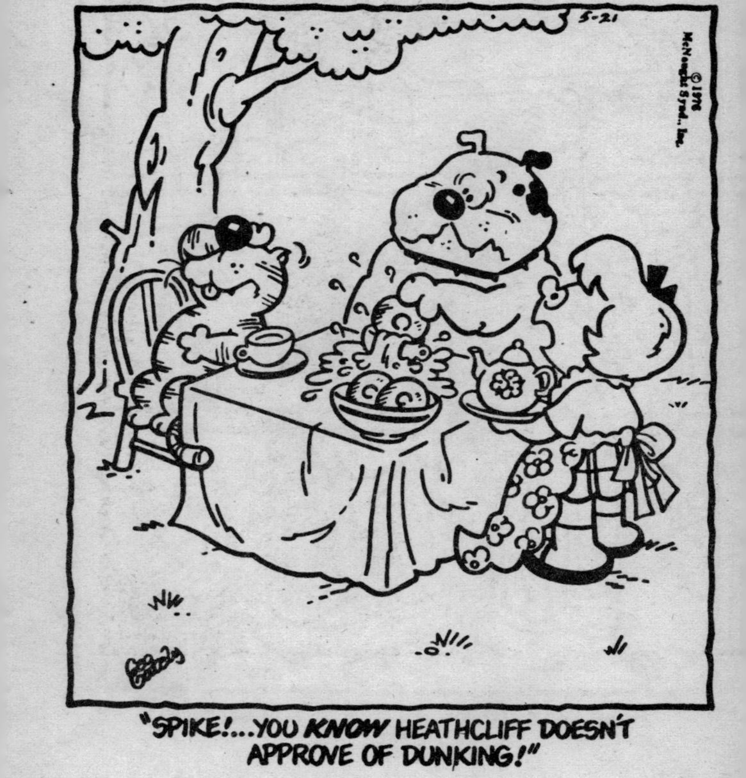
5-21
© 1978
McNaught Synd., Inc.

"SPIKE!...YOU ***KNOW*** HEATHCLIFF DOESN'T APPROVE OF DUNKING!"

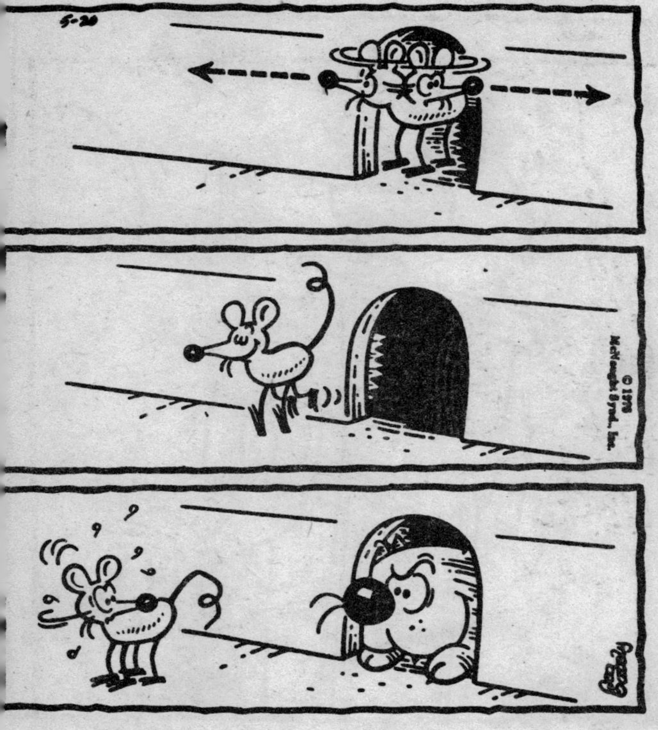
5-20
© 1978
McNaught Synd., Inc.

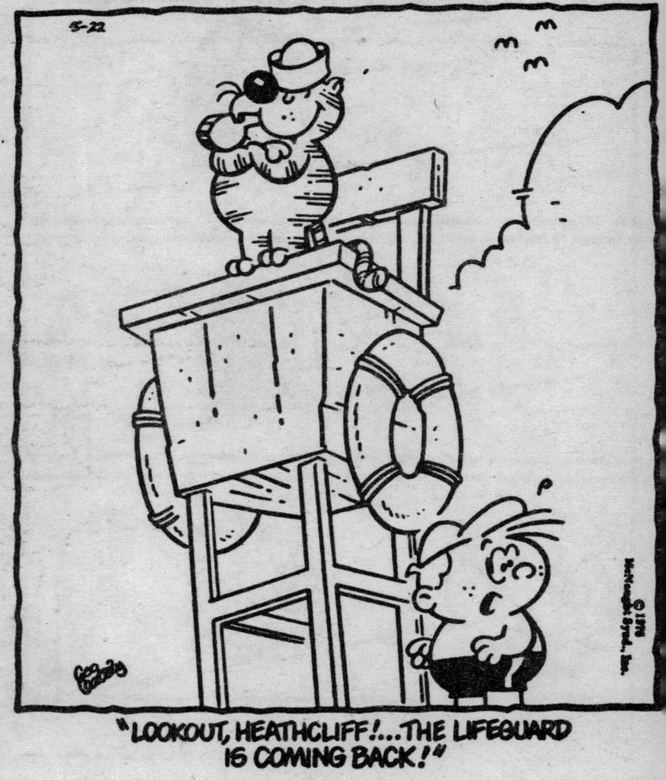
5-22
© 1978 McNaught Synd., Inc.

"LOOKOUT, HEATHCLIFF!...THE LIFEGUARD IS COMING BACK!"

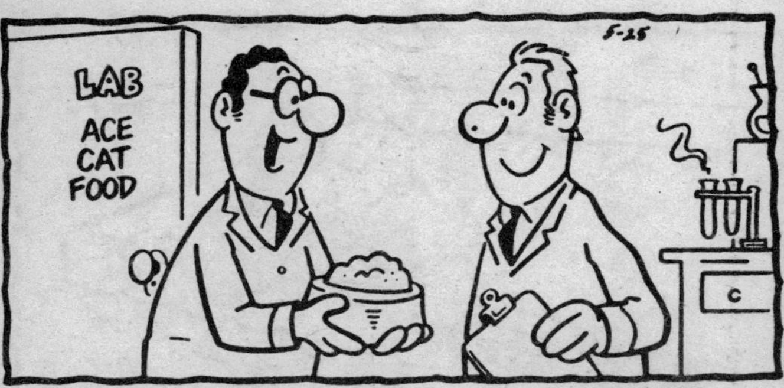
LAB
ACE
CAT
FOOD
5-25

"IT'S A GREAT NEW CAT FOOD!...NOW, IF I CAN JUST GET AN OKAY FROM 'QUALITY CONTROL'..."

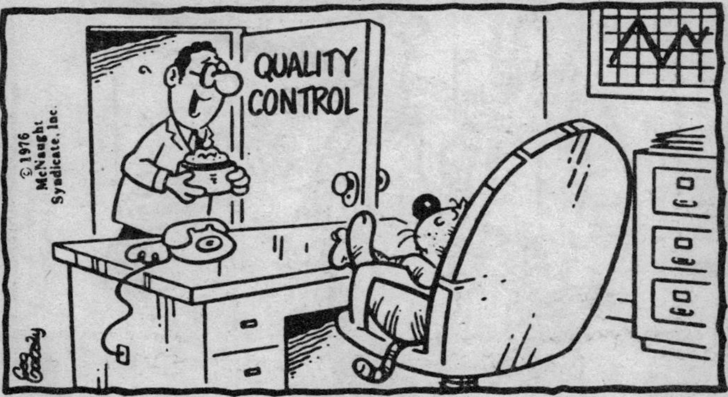
QUALITY
CONTROL
© 1976
McNaught
Syndicate, Inc.

"BUSY?"

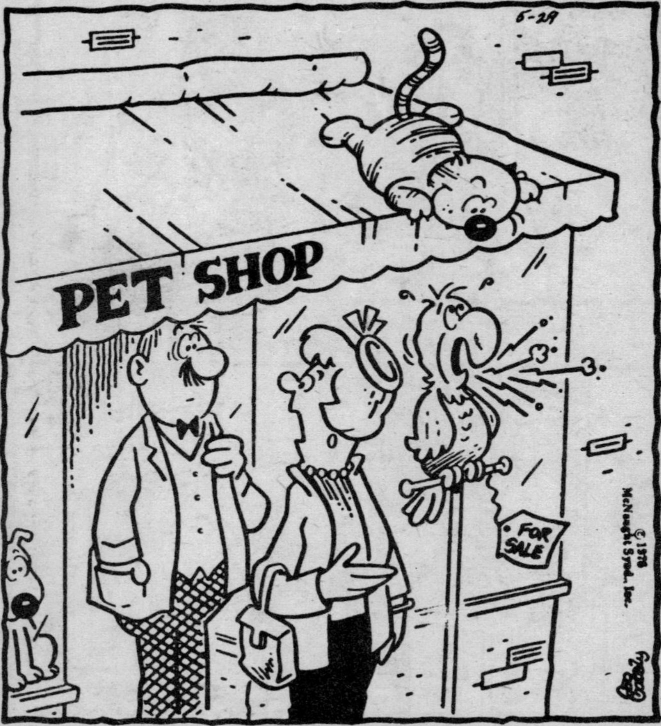
5-29
PET SHOP
FOR SALE
© 1978 McNaught Synd., Inc.

"IS THAT ALL HE CAN SAY?... 'THE SKY IS FALLING!'?"

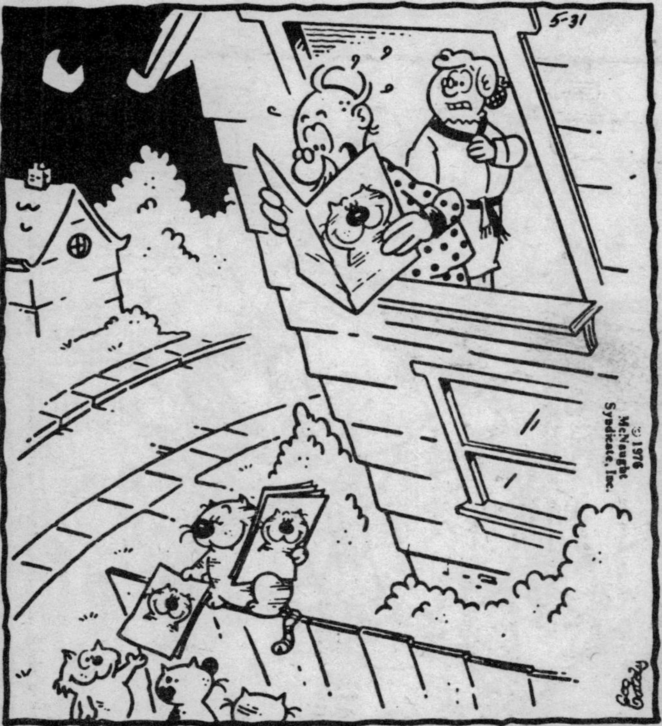
5-31
© 1976 McNaught Syndicate, Inc.

"OH, BROTHER!...WAIT'LL YOU SEE THE PROGRAM FOR TONIGHT'S CONCERT!"

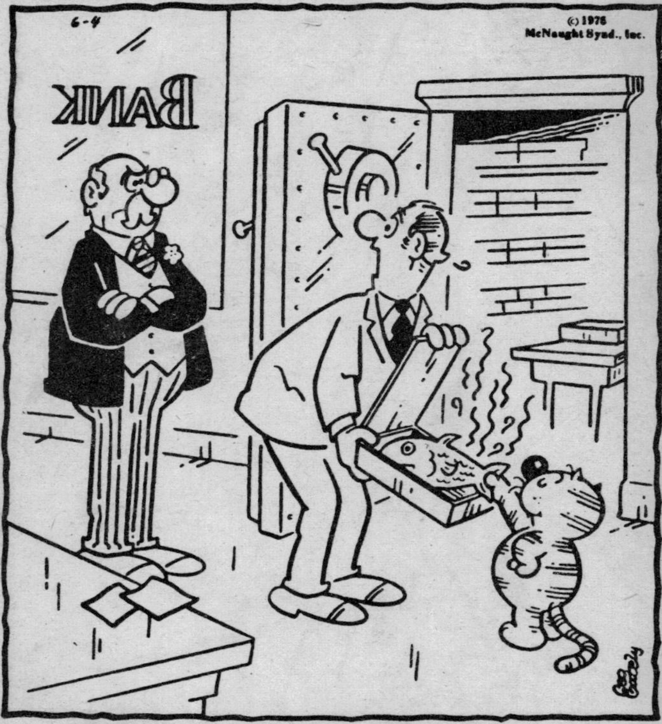
6-4
BANK
(c) 1976
McNaught Synd., Inc.

"WHAT CAN I DO?!...IT'S HIS OWN SAFETY DEPOSIT BOX!"